FABULOUS
FELTED
SCARVES

FABULOUS
FELTED
SCARVES

20 WEARABLE WORKS OF ART

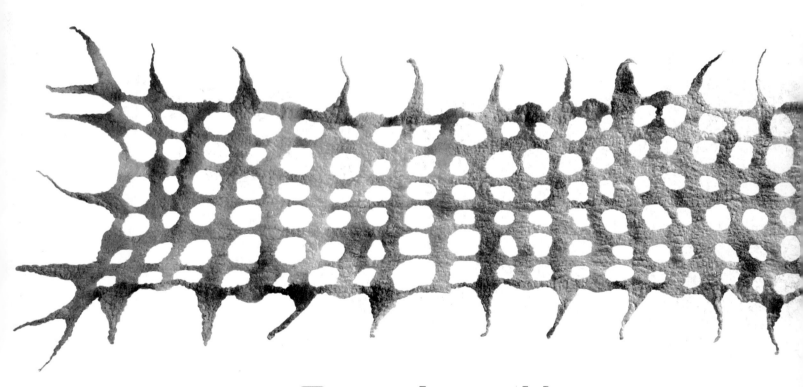

CHAD ALICE HAGEN
JORIE JOHNSON

LARK BOOKS
A Division of Sterling Publishing Co., Inc.
New York / London

Editor: Linda Kopp

Art Director: Dana Irwin

Cover Designer: Cindy LaBreacht

Assistant Editor: Susan Keiffer

Associate Art Director: Avery Johnson

Art Production Assistant:
Jeff Hamilton

Editorial Assistance:
Mark Bloom, Cassie Moore

Photographer: John Widman

Illustrations: Orrin Lundgren

Hair & Makeup: Scott Thompson

Library of Congress Cataloging-in-Publication Data

Hagen, Chad Alice.
  Fabulous felted scarves : 20 wearable works of art / Chad Alice Hagen,
Jorie Johnson. -- 1st ed.
      p. cm.
  Includes index.
  ISBN-13: 978-1-60059-002-3 (hc-plc with jacket : alk. paper)
  ISBN-10: 1-60059-002-0 (hc-plc with jacket : alk. paper)
  1. Scarves. 2. Felt work. I. Johnson, Jorie. II. Title.
  TT667.5.H33 2007
  746'.0463--dc22
                                              2007011110

10 9 8 7 6 5 4 3 2 1

First Edition

Published by Lark Books, A Division of
Sterling Publishing Co., Inc.
387 Park Avenue South, New York, N.Y. 10016

Text © 2007, Chad Alice Hagen, Jorie Johnson
Photography © 2007, Lark Books
Illustrations © 2007, Lark Books

Distributed in Canada by Sterling Publishing,
c/o Canadian Manda Group, 165 Dufferin Street
Toronto, Ontario, Canada M6K 3H6

Distributed in the United Kingdom by GMC Distribution Services,
Castle Place, 166 High Street, Lewes, East Sussex, England BN7 1XU

Distributed in Australia by Capricorn Link (Australia) Pty Ltd.,
P.O. Box 704, Windsor, NSW 2756 Australia

If you have questions or comments about this book, please contact:
Lark Books
67 Broadway
Asheville, NC 28801
(828) 253-0467

Manufactured in China

ISBN 13: 978-1-60059-002-3
ISBN 10: 1-60059-002-0

For information about custom editions, special sales, premium and corporate
purchases, please contact Sterling Special Sales Department at 800-805-5489 or
specialsales@sterlingpub.com.

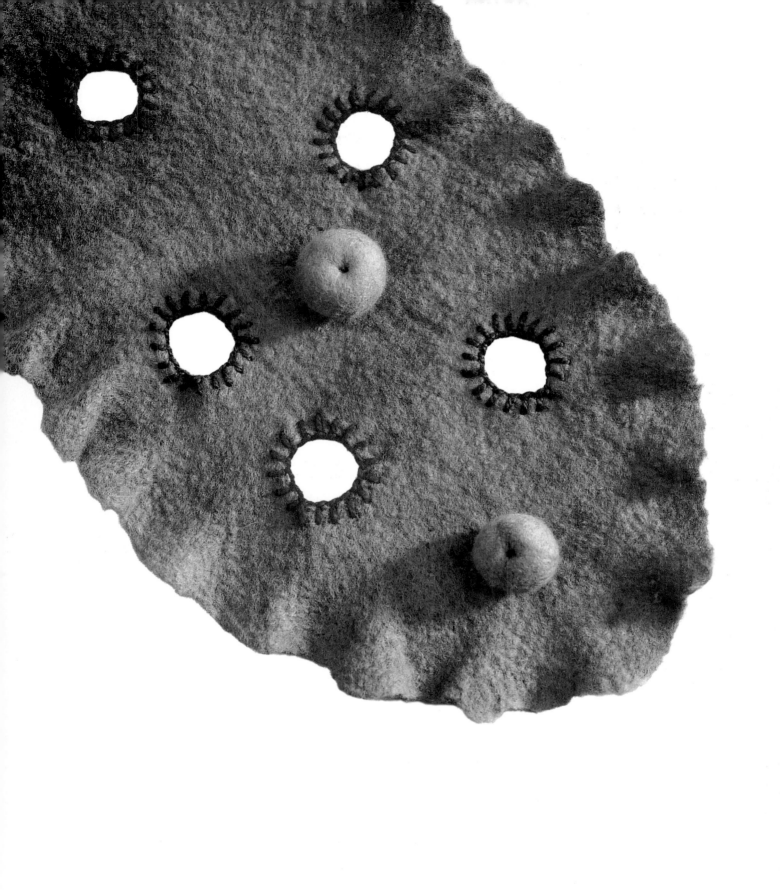

INTRODUCTION ... 8

BASICS .. 10

Feltmaking Tools and Supplies 10

Layout and Felting 15

3-D Basics ... 25

Dyeing ... 30

Carding ... 36

Flat Braiding ... 38

PROJECTS
DESIGNS BY CHAD

Airy Fairy Scarf ... 44

Mr. Saturday Night ... 47

Boa Boa ... 50

Bark Scarf ... 54

Blackbeard ... 58

Inge's Fancy ... 62

Dread Nauts ... 65

Lily Pad Wrap ... 68

Magic Muffler ... 72

Bubble Boa ... 77

DESIGNS BY JORIE

94 .... Dip Dyed Party Scarf

99 .... Fallen Leaves Collar

104 .... Father's Day Braided Muffler

108 .... Honeycomb Scarf

112 .... Granny Warner's Lace Shawl

117 .... Wedding Stole

122 ... Lei Collar

126 .... Link Muffler Series

131 ... Chalk Drawings Muffler

136 .... Snow People Scarf

139 .... Rainbow Ribbons

80 ... GALLERY

141 ... ACKNOWLEDGEMENTS

140 ... ABOUT THE AUTHORS

143 ... INDEX

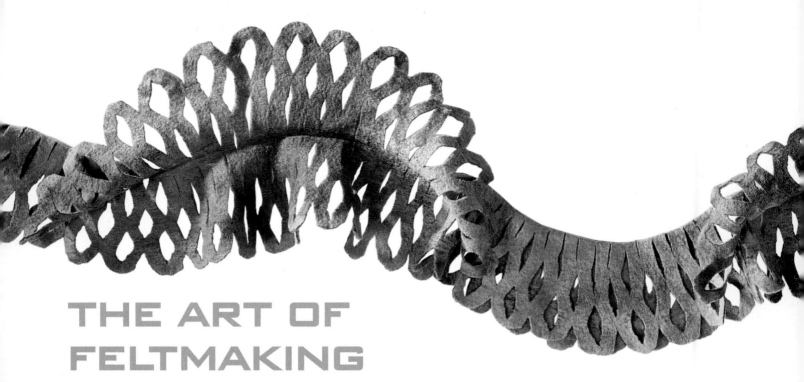

THE ART OF FELTMAKING

In this book you'll meet two artists with two ways of seeing the world and changing the unseen into visible form. They both pick up curled locks of wool and lay down layers of even fleece. They dip their hands into warm soapy water and join into a partnership with the wool to form a supple, coherent textile.

Clothing, accessories, and interior felt works designed by Jorie are infused with the nuances of color and the delicate shapes and lines of her adopted countries of Finland and Japan. Chad Alice, as an American working artist, teaches and experiments with color and surface. Between them they have five decades of working with wool—taking it into their studios and lives—making it entangle, dance, and evolve.

Why did they decide to present these techniques through the felted scarf? The flat plane and relative size of a scarf presents a perfect canvas for experimentation and understanding. Also, there is the challenge of making finer wool felt fabrics—taking the feltmaker from the discovery of wool and water to an awareness of how to manipulate the fiber. How thin can you make it? What happens if you succeed? Is it a better scarf? Is it interesting?

This book, while paying homage to the generations of feltmakers, workshops, and written words, wishes to fuse the ancient craft of working with wool with contemporary, creative inspiration. You, the reader/craftsperson may now benefit and learn from the experiences and discoveries of these two very different felt designers. Journey with them as they explore a wide range of felting techniques sure to increase your own skills, while stimulating and inspiring the creative thought process.

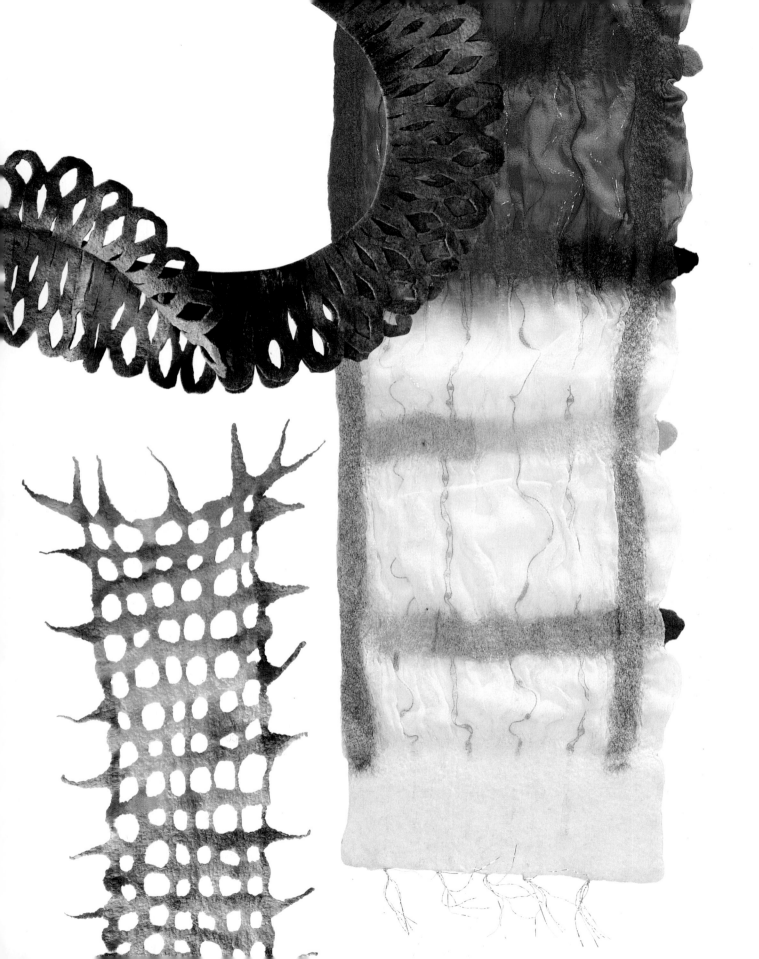

FELTING BASICS

FELTMAKING TOOLS AND SUPPLIES

When you come right down to it, feltmaking chiefly requires wool, water, and soap. You'll also need some basic felting equipment and auxiliary supplies, but in most cases these items can be found around the house or acquired inexpensively. Start your collection today and add to it as you move on to new techniques. The following lists of basic tools and supplies will help get you off to a good start.

THE BASIC BASICS

Wool

There are many different types of wool and fibers with which to make beautiful scarves. Every sheep breed produces wool with different characteristics; therefore, it is necessary to take some time to learn about the wool you are using. These days it is easy to buy beautifully dyed and combed wool in rope-like cords (called roving), and sheet forms (batts), so starting a project becomes a breeze. It is essential to start with well-washed and carded materials, which are readily available from many spinning, weaving, and wool supply shops, as well as from the numerous websites selling feltmaking materials.

If you would prefer to use wool from

Worktable and Covers

A sturdy table is essential. For ease of working, generally the table height should be 3 to 6 inches (7.6 to 15.2 cm) below your bent elbow. To save your back, consider raising the table by placing its legs on blocks of wood or in lengths of PVC pipes.

Waterproof covers for your worktable are good for controlling wet areas. They can be purchased by the yard in many fabric stores. It is handy to have a few covers: one white or light colored for laying out dark wools, and another black or dark gray for laying out light colored wools. Large sheets of heavy plastic are also good for drawing out patterns with permanent markers if you don't want to mark on your other covers.

To make your feet and legs more comfortable during layout and felting, it helps to wear sturdy shoes and stand on a heavy rubber mat.

your own sheep or those of a friend, make sure it is well washed, dried, and carded before starting.

Water

A ready source of hot water is important for mixing up soapy water solutions and for rinsing. If you have hard water, add a ½ teaspoon (2.5 mL) of water softener to your bucket.

Soap

Soap is a vital element to the felting process. In a soapy solution, the soap helps to quickly wet the fibers and change the pH of the felting wool to a condition that enables the scales to fully expand from the shaft of the wool fiber. It also aids the fibers in sliding past each other during the agitation process, and helps your hands to move smoothly over the wool surface.

Chad uses grated or chopped olive oil bar soap dissolved in warm water to make a thick solution. For most of her scarf projects, the soapy water used is made from about ½ cup of the thick soap solution whisked into a gallon of warm water. Exact amounts are not important, but look for a good soapy feel when you rub your fingers together in the solution.

Jorie prefers a teaspoon (5 mL) of colorless, non-conditioned shampoo added to a 20 oz (600 mL) bottle of hot water. For more specifics as to Jorie's recommended pH solution, see Felting Solution on page 22.

When additional soap suds need to be added directly to the felt, both Chad and Jorie use a bar of natural olive oil soap.

PVC pipes and worktable coverings.

Below are described three different groups of tools for the scarves in this book. The Basic Felting Kit will be used for almost all the scarves in this book; Chad's Additional Felting Tools and Jorie's Additional Felting Tools are lists of tools that are very useful for working with their specific designs and instructions.

BASIC FELTING KIT

Notepad for sketching, notes, and calculations

Pens, pencils, drawing tools for notes and ideas

Felting solution (made with water and soap or shampoo)

Sharp scissors

Calculator

Permanent marker

Tape measure

Sewing kit (a basic kit with various needles and thread, pins, etc.)

Vinegar

Scale with metric function in 0.1 delineations (use a balance postage, or digital one for measuring small amounts of wool and dye, and a kitchen scale for larger amounts).

Plastic bottle with holes pierced in the cap, rubber squeeze ball, small dipper cup, or any similar device for wetting wool

Bar of soap

Towels

Kitchen-type sponges (no "scrubbie" sides)

Buckets and basins

Waterproof apron

Steam iron

CHAD'S ADDITIONAL FELTING TOOLS

Whisk for mixing soap and water

Plastic bags to keep scarves damp for resist work

Two-part ridged plastic felt mat (the type of mat often used for drawer liners, with a sticky mat placed underneath to prevent sliding). Used for rolling 3D tails and ropes.

Large sheets of plastic or paper to trace patterns

White pencil or white tailor's chalk for use on dark surfaces

Yardstick for measuring out the layout patterns

Small sharp scissors

Small dowel for rolling and flattening edges of finished scarf

Sushi mat to hard roll felted rope, tails, etc.

Counting stones*

*Counting stones are five small stones and a small plastic container. They help you maintain the count of the various types of agitation that you will be using on the scarf. It works! Try it. Place the container and stones at one end of the scarf. When you do the specific agitation, *once down the scarf and then back to the beginning,* put a stone in the container. Continue. When the required number of stones are in the plastic container, you are finished with that part of the agitation.

JORIE'S ADDITIONAL FELTING TOOLS

Small bamboo mat or glass washboard, for making all sizes of cords.

Bubble wrap with small (⅜-inch-diameter [9.5 mm]) bubble surface for laying your wool out on while rolling the project during the shrinking process)

Polyester mesh for stabilizing the designs while wetting the wool

Rolling rods (wooden dowel, plastic pipe, stainless pipe, polystyrene or dense foam rubber pipe insulation covering, etc.) of various diameters and lengths depending on the need (up to 1⅝ inch [4 cm] diameter)

Old sheet or cotton fabric to bind the rolling bundle securely and to absorb excess felting solution

Ties, such as old nylon knee-highs, wide rubber bands, or shoelaces to secure a bundle for rolling

Small soft plastic bags to slip over your hands while rubbing the surface of the wet wool

Painter's plastic, or any thin, flexible plastic sheeting that causes a vacuum between the bubble wrap and wool to stabilize the fibers and assist in the shrinking process

Miscellaneous Tools

(Needed for some of Jorie's specific projects)

Wide roll of paper

Hand spinner's hand carders for blending colored wool or different fibers (a pair of soft wire-toothed pet brushes may be substituted)

Giant 1¼-inch-diameter (3.2 cm) bubble wrap is used for maintaining pattern spacing in the making of **Honeycomb Scarf** (see page 108)

Mist bottle for dampening

Vinegar to prepare a mild rinse to return the pH of silk and wool back to their original acid count

Hair conditioner to soften and silken the wool fibers in the final rinse stage of the work

Needle-nose pilers to straighten felt edges

Fork to arrange details of a design

Small brush to open clumps of fiber

Electric sander (used without sandpaper). See Selecting a Sander (page 14)

Felting needles #36

SELECTING A SANDER

You will find using a sander very useful in facilitating the felting process; I used one for the **Father's Day Muffler** and the **Wedding Stole**. Electric sanders are not meant to be used around water, so be sure to follow the safety precautions listed below.

When selecting a sander, look for a flat-bed model with a solid urethane sponge bottom plate (or cover the bottom of the sander with a sponge yourself). Get a cheaper model that is not too heavy and does not have a vacuum system for dust removal. I generally use a $3\frac{1}{2}$ x $7\frac{1}{2}$-inch (8.9 x 19 cm) flat-bed sander.

SANDER SAFETY

- Wear rubber-soled shoes and thick rubber gloves.

- Plug the sander into an extension cord with a ground fault interrupter (GFI), or into a GFI outlet.

- Keep the floor dry where you are standing.

- Before starting, remove excess moisture from the wool by blotting with a towel.

CHAD'S

LAYOUT & FELTING BASICS

The wool you will be using for making some of the scarves in this book should be already processed into roving—or sliver—a thick rope of wool. The wool has been washed and cleaned of all vegetable matter, dirt, and oils, and has been put through a carding machine that straightens and combs the wool fibers so they are all lying in the same direction. The Merino that I am using is in a roving form, but all the smaller fibers have been dropped out during the carding process so it is called top.

Thin, even layers are the foundation of each of my scarves. Learning how to lay out the wool layers skillfully takes some practice, time, and patience. If you are not familiar with working with fine Merino, take a few minutes and lay out a sample. Remember: THIN is the operative word! Trying to rush a project by using long, thick pieces of wool will only create uneven and thick scarves.

THE WOOLS I USE

I am using several different wools for my scarf projects in this book: a 22–24 top Merino, a fine Merino wool of 17 microns, a commercially made Merino needle felt batt, a 50/50 blend of merino and wild tussah silk, Mohair locks, and huacaya alpaca. All of these wools produce a soft and flexible scarf, yet each one lends a different look and feel to the scarf. Although any of the above wools can be used with any scarf technique, I am including my recommendations for each project.

The Merino top is a wonderful wool that I have used for just about anything wearable. It is a fast felter, soft, yet gives a bit

of body to the scarf that is perfect for resist-shaped projects and 3D elements. I will be using this for the **Bubble Boa** (page 77), the **Bark Scarf** (page 54), **Dread Nauts** (page 65), and **Lily Pad Wrap** (page 68). The center of the **Boa Boa** wrap (page 50) is created from the Merino with fabulous, soft Mohair locks added for the fringe.

The 17-micron Merino is becoming very popular in the felting world for its incredible softness and density of the felted surface. I will be using this wool for **Inge's Fancy** (page 62) and the **Airy Fairy Scarf** (page 44).

The **Blackbeard** scarf (page 58) is made from commercially needle-felted Merino prefelt. This is made from Merino fleece laid in layers on a needle-felting machine, which entangles the wool fibers by punching them with thousands of barbed needles, producing a strong and dense "prefelt" ready for the final fulling and felting.

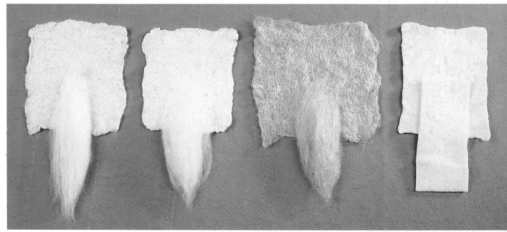

| Merino top 22–24 micron | Fine Merino 17 micron | 50% tussah silk 50% Merino | Needle prefelt Merino |

The 50/50 Merino/wild tussah silk blend is a natural for dyeing, as the shiny silk fibers contrast beautifully with the dense Merino. Since the blend has so much silk, it felts quickly and creates a great textured surface, thanks to the long, curled silk fibers. This blend is used for the **Magic Muffler** project (page 72).

The growing interest in llama and alpaca fibers inspired my **Mr. Saturday Night** scarf (page 47). This handsome two-toned scarf is felted from a luscious huacaya alpaca fiber roving.

BASIC WOOL LAYOUT

1 Hold a length of merino roving and pull it apart into equal halves (photo 1). Merino fiber is very long (3 to 6 inches [7.6 to 15.2 cm]), so place your hands about 5 to 6 inches (12.7 to 15.2 cm) away from each other, before gently pulling the fibers in half. Make sure the roving is not twisted, as even a single twist makes it almost impossible to pull the wool apart.

2 Estimate where the center is and divide one of the lengths of roving cleanly into equal halves with your thumbs and forefingers (photo 2).

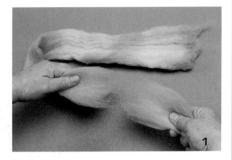

3 Continue to pull off and divide the roving until you get the size and thickness of pieces that are as long as your hand. This is the size and amount of Merino wool that you will use to lay out the "shingles".

4 As shown in photo 4, hold the small length of roving in your right hand pinched between your thumb and the side of your forefinger (if left-handed, reverse the hand instructions). Lay the other end of the roving on the table, and place your left hand with fingers flat over the very end of the roving. Hold your fingers down as you pull with the right hand, and a very thin, even "shingle" of wool will pull out easily. Pat this "shingle" down very gently with your hand before moving on. I call this "Pat the Bunny."

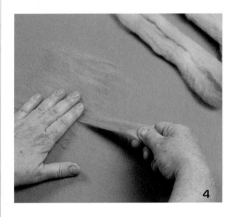

Laying Out One Layer

Continue to lay out these small, thin shingles of wool side by side in the same direction, overlapping the thin tops and bottoms like shingles on a roof, until you have covered the area required for your project. If you have any wool left over, go back over the layer "patting the bunny" until you feel areas that need more wool. Use all the wool designated for that layer.

Each scarf will be constructed of two to four layers of wool according to their individual instructions.

LAYING OUT AND FELTING THE SCARF

This method for laying out layers of fine wool for scarves is simple and direct. Since the wool is very fine, make sure all fans are off, that doors and windows are closed, and don't sneeze or walk fast around the laid-out wool.

Use this method with the following scarf projects:

Inge's Fancy

Bubble Boa

Lily Pad Wrap (four layers)

Bark Scarf

Magic Muffler

Boa Boa (steps 1 to 13 only)

Mr. Saturday Night

Supplies

(Also see Basic Felting Kit on page 12)

Waterproof cover on worktable (light cover for medium to dark wool colors, and black or dark gray cover for white and light wool colors)

Waterproof marker (tailor's chalk or white pencil for dark cover)

Yardstick

Required amount of wool for your project

Instructions

1 Check scarf instructions for dimensions, and using a ruler and a marker (or chalk), measure and draw out the pattern for your scarf on the table cover (photo 5). To allow for a working space, start the measurement 3 to 4 inches (7.6 to 10.2 cm) up from the edge of the table. If you don't want to permanently mark your table, cover the working surface with heavy plastic.

2 Divide the roving into two, three, or four equal sections as noted in scarf directions. Each of these sections will be for one layer of the scarf.

3 Layer one: Divide the first section of roving into small workable sections. Create the first layer by laying out the wool along the drawn lines, then filling the center horizontally, from left to right if right-handed (photo 6). Use all the wool of the first section.

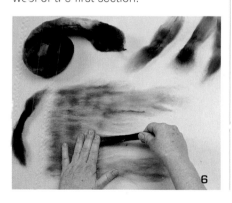

4 The second layer: Divide the next section of roving into small pieces, and lay out the layer vertically, from top to bottom, extending about 1 inch (2.5 cm) beyond the top and bottom edges of the pattern (photo 7).

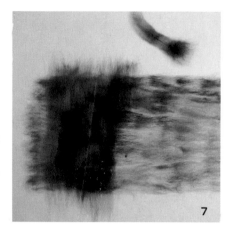

5 Tuck under any wool extending beyond the pattern lines until they are even with the lines (photo 8). Pat gently and adjust to make a straight edge. Fold over the extra wool on the left and right edges of the scarf.

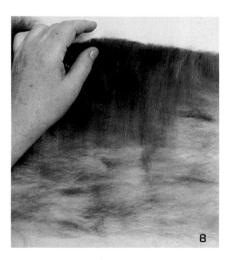

6 If the directions call for fringe, or you want to add some, pull off shingles of wool along the long edges of the scarf as shown in photo 9.

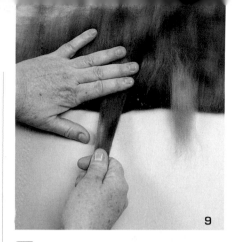

7 Use the third section of roving to lay out a third layer perpendicular to the second layer (photo 10). Lay out the wool left to right just like you did for the first layer. If you have any fringe, this layer will cover the ends.

8 Dry felting helps compress the wool fibers prior to wetting, and actually helps speed up the felting process. To dry felt the scarf, lay both of your hands with outstretched fingers on the laid-out wool. Gently move the whole scarf up and down against the tabletop (photo 11, page 18). Do not move the *surface* of the scarf, move the *whole piece*. Count to five while moving the scarf and then move your hands to the next untouched section. Continue until you have dry felted the length of the scarf twice (1 stone).

Now we will start the felting process with soapy water, sponges, towels, rubber balls, water bucket, and counting stones (Basic Felting Kit, page 12).

9 Set up your tools next to your laid-out scarf. Fill the rubber ball sprayer from the soapy water bucket and spray the laid-out scarf, wetting the edges first and then the center (photo 12). Use lots of water.

10 Gently pat the wetted scarf with flat, outstretched fingers only, not the palms of your hands, making sure all areas are saturated (photo 13). The wool is totally saturated when it seems to stick to the table and turn a darker color. Add more water from the spray bottle as needed. Pat the wet felt for four passes (two stones).

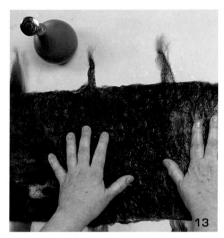

11 If you have added fringe, rub them into thin strips by holding the scarf end of the fringe with one hand and lightly rubbing the fringe once or twice with a sponge until it rolls together (photo 14).

12 The sharpei rub, named after the wrinkled dog, is done by using both your hands, one above the other. Use your whole hand, the palm with fingers outstretched to support the wool (photo 15). The scarf needs to be very wet when doing this, so add more water. You will be gently rubbing the wool against the table, up and down only (just like the dry felting), wrinkling the felt as you rub, for the count of five. Leave the wrinkles in when you move from one place to the next. Try to cover every bit of the scarf. Move slowly and thoughtfully, and watch what happens. Remember: always move your hands in an up-and-down motion, because if you move side to side you will stretch huge holes in the scarf. Sharpei rub the wet wool for five stones (10 passes).

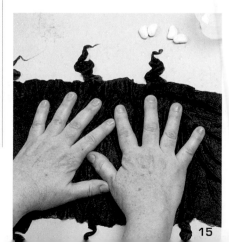

13 Press sponges against the wet scarf to remove excess water, and squeeze them into a wastewater tub (photo 16). If you have fringe, snip the tiny ends off with scissors.

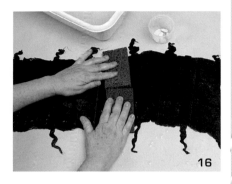

14 Push both ends of the scarf to the center of your work area (photo 17).

15 Gently pick up the scarf with both hands and very gently squeeze 25 times into the wastewater tub (photo 18). You should squeeze so gently that you will still have water dripping out even at the 25th squeeze.

16 Put the wet scarf into the soapy water bucket and lightly "lingerie wash," swishing it around for a few moments. Remove and gently squeeze out about half the water.

Throwing is a fast and useful method of fulling (heavily felting) the scarf as the vibrations caused by throwing the wet scarf down hard against the tabletop help move the wool fibers closer together. It also helps you stretch out your back. Use both hands to throw the scarf down so you don't pull any muscles (photo 19). When you throw the scarf down hard it should make a loud thump. If not, either add more water to the scarf or throw harder. If you have too much water in a scarf, you will splash yourself and your studio. Squeeze out the excess.

17 Throw the scarf gently 25 times.

18 Open the scarf completely, without stretching any part of it, and examine the edges for any folds; or if you have fringe, make sure all the fringe is loose and not starting to felt into the scarf (photo 20). Push the scarf together from the ends again.

19 Repeat steps 16, 17, and 18 two more times, throwing the scarf harder the second and third times.

20 "Knead and throw" instead of throwing for two more sequences (repeating steps 16, 17, and 18). For this agitation, knead the scarf like bread dough for a count of five and then toss. Repeat 25 times.

21 Small pebbles will start to form on the surface of the scarf (photo 21). When this happens all over your scarf, it is felted enough. Rinse the scarf under hot water until all the soap is gone, and then squeeze it in a **vinegar rinse** *(1 cup [.24 L] vinegar to 1 gallon (3.8 L) water or 1 Tbsp [15 mL] of citric acid to ½ gallon [1.9 L] water)* a few times to neutralize any remaining soap. Wrap scarf in a towel, place on the floor, and step on the towel to remove more water.

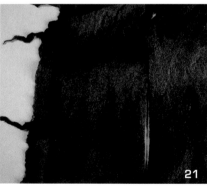

21

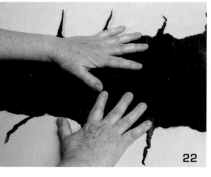

22

22 Lay scarf back on a clean, dry worktable, then flatten and straighten the edges. You can use pliers to get a straighter edge. Pull on fringes to straighten. For wrinkled edges, try rolling the damp scarf up on a dowel and alternate squeezing the edges and then rolling the whole thing for several minutes. Unroll, and try rolling the dowel over the edges (photo 23).

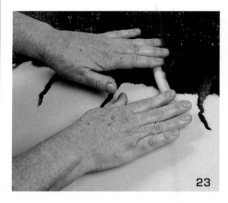

23

NOTE: *If you will be dyeing the scarf, roll it up and place it in a plastic bag, as it needs to stay wet until it is folded, tied, and dyed. If you will not be able to do the dyeing within five hours, then dry the scarf and rewet it in warm water for 20 minutes before dyeing it.*

I usually let the scarf dry either on the table or, after an hour, I'll fold it over a hanger to finish drying. When dry, iron the scarf for a nice flat finish (photo 24).

24

JORIE'S

LAYOUT & FELTING BASICS

THE WOOLS I USED

Wool availability has come a long way since having to raise your own animal to get what you need. With the aid of the internet you can now order whatever you desire. A relatively inexpensive material at the start, wool gets costlier as it gets processed—especially if you order from a foreign country and must pay additional delivery charges. When I first moved to Japan (which is nothing like the wool countries of Europe), I had to rely on imported wool.

Now there are more possibilities to order wool within Japan. When traveling, I always source wool, sometimes directly from the shepherd. That way I can get the quality, color, and item prepared to my specific needs.

For many of the projects in this book I used readily accessible wools: 64 Merino and 58 crossbred—the traditional standbys. But in the case of the **Father's Day Braided Muffler** (page 104) I added a silk/Merino blend, and my **Granny Warner's Lace Shawl** (page 112) uses lustrous wool called English Leicester. Also, I introduce incorporating mohair knitting yarns in **Chalk Drawings Muffler** (page 131), and for an alternative effect I substituted laces and strips of silk fabric for some of the carded wool to make the perfect **Wedding Stole** (page 117).

Dyed wool comes in all colors, but if you can't find your favorite brownish red, consider learning how to enhance store-bought colors. This can be accomplished by either color mixing them with a pair of hand carders, as was done in **Fallen Leaves Collar** (page 99), or by learning how to layer colors, resulting in them self-blending during the shrinking process, as in **Rainbow Ribbons** (page 139).

I generally keep my range for scarves between 58s and 80s (27.5 and 18.5 micron). Although felt as a fabric can be very

strong, each individual fiber is a delicate filament that can be overworked, making it lose its sheen and look worn. To avoid this condition, strive to shrink the wool JUST to the point of being ready rather than over-stressing it. Since you are trying to make a flexible fabric to be wrapped around the neck, it can be slightly less densely felted. My suggestion is to work the wool until you can no longer see in which direction the last layer was laid down. This ensures that the fibers have sufficiently entangled.

Keep in mind that for a neck wrap with the softest hand and supple drape you should look for wool with a higher quality

English Leicester washed fleece surrounded by Merino top.

count and smaller micron diameter. Remember that the finer the wool (identified by a higher Bradford Quality Count (UK) or lower Southern Hemisphere micron), the smaller the wool diameter is and the softer and more flexible the fiber. It is possible to combine different breeds of wool as well as wool fineness. For example, both 58's and 64's qualities appear together in some instructions, like the **Snow People Scarf** on page 136.

When making scarves you must concentrate on making especially thin and supple felt fabrics comparable to woven fabrics and knits. This is a challenge for the beginner as well as the seasoned felter. Learning how to use your fingers in new ways will take some concentration at the start. Practice truly makes perfect when it comes to these thinner fabrics.

BASIC WOOL LAYOUT

Using wool in either roving (rope-like combed fibers aligned in the same direction and ready for spinning into yarn) or batt form (carded into wider sheet forms) is fine as long as the required amount of wool is not exceeded and the measured quantity is optimally used.

Instructions

1 Separate the roving into convenient, narrower strands before starting. Normally fourths or sixths is fine. Wool company equipment varies as does their product, thus the diameter of top will vary as well. You will soon learn for yourself how to handle your local brand depending on the way it has been processed.

2 Spread a strand of divided roving to the width of four fingers, and pull the very tips off by pressing them between your four fingertips and the palm of your hand (photo 25). This will

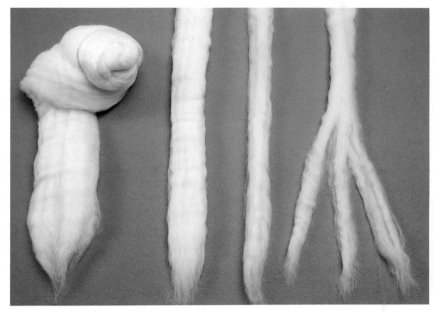

From left: 64 tops, ½ strand, ¼ strand, division of ¼ strand into thirds (making ¹⁄₁₂ strands)

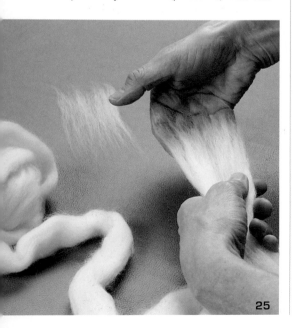

25

result in an even cloud-like layer rather than pulling off a narrower bit between two fingers. Make sure to position your opposite hand at an appropriate distance that offers enough tension to the rope end, thereby regulating the amount of wool pulled off the strand at one time. Too loose of a hold will cause little control over the quantity, and too tight of a hold will cause your hands to tire. The length of the fibers vary with the breeds, so you may well find yourself holding the top at different distances, depending on the product.

3 Pull off the next section of cloud and lay it next to the first, continuing with the required wool for each layer. Ration the wool so that you use, for example, a third of it in one-third of the area to be covered. You are perfecting your finer felt skill, which requires constant checking that the weighed wool is optimally used.

WETTING PROCEDURE: FELTING SOLUTION, NETS

Felting Solution

Wool will not felt on its own. A major factor in the process is the felting solution. There are four major factors that coax a state of change among the fibers: heat, moisture, soap, and change of pH. Later on we will discuss the other components such as friction, pressure, time, and enthusiasm—which, together, aid in the production of a perfectly felted object.

To make the long history of feltmaking shorter, it is necessary to change the pH of the wool fiber toward either an acid or alkaline (base) condition. For hand-felting, alkaline solution is preferred as it is far safer to use. Acid-based felting is better left to the automated machinery of factory production. A teaspoon of shampoo (preferably colorless and non-conditioned) added to a 20-oz (600 mL) bottle full of hot water (about 110°F or 44°C) is enough to push the pH of the water toward 8–9 on the scale.

You must take into consideration the hardness or softness of the water you'll be using, as it will dictate the amount (greater or lesser) of shampoo or liquid soap needed. Practically speaking, the pH of the fiber needs to be changed from the 4.9 of the wool to a higher (or lower) pH in order for the outer surface of cuticles to roughen, as well as to lubricate the fibers so sliding increases. Too much lather will create a lot of air between the fibers, preventing them from interlocking and entangling, which is essentially our goal.

It is safe to say that every teacher has a different preferred felting solution depending on country, tradition, convenience, and personal skin conditions. Try out a few alternatives before choosing your standard solution.

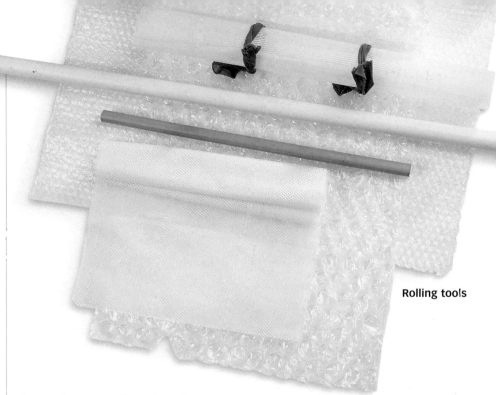

Rolling tools

Nets

Using a net to stabilize the design area and fibers is wise when wetting your fine work. A net such as the polyester mesh fabric used for sportswear, coated door screening, pressed plastic net, or even an old lace curtain will come in handy. Different materials can be used for different objects, as some materials are more flexible and stretch more than others.

Carefully lay the net over a portion or all of the prepared fibers (photo 26). After wetting the wool, be careful how you lift off the net so you don't disturb any of your design, or pull off any fibers that might have become caught in the mesh.

There are many ways to coax fibers to move and activate entangling, resulting in shrinkage. These include hand massage (photo 27), rolling between both hands, forearm or feet rolling (with or without a rod), throwing onto a tabletop, kneading, and using a clothes washer, clothes dryer, or a sanding machine. Three of the more important

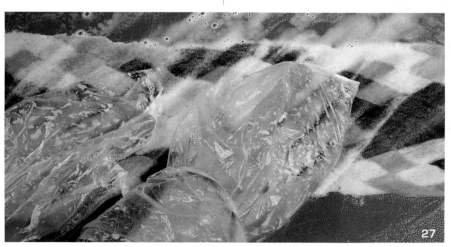

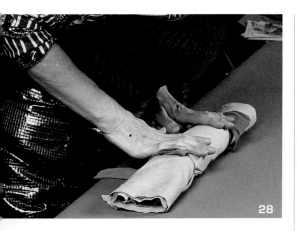

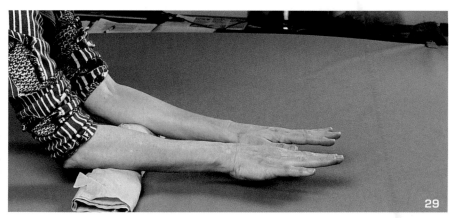

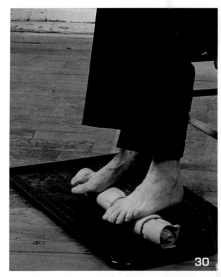

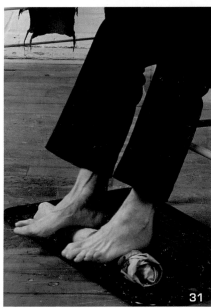

reasons why wool turns into felt include: agitation, pressure, and duration of treatment.

The differences in agitation action should be noted, as sometimes more than one technique is used during the making of a single project. Usually you will be instructed to start out gently, and once the fibers have started to attach or entangle with each other, then add more pressure and utilize a slightly rougher strategy, encouraging further shrinking and resulting in a finer-quality felt fabric.

Hand massaging, repeated rolling around a rod or plastic pipe, and throwing are commonly used methods and are illustrated in the following sequence of pictures.

Hand Massaging

People tend to want to caress the soapy surface, which is a natural psychological human reaction, but some delicate designs make it impossible to begin by stroking. Rolling helps to interlock the fibers fastest, all across the surface at the same time. To assist some otherwise uninitiated fibers to move a bit more, I employ hand massage to coax the area into shape.

Whenever you read in my project instructions to "use your hands to massage the wool," always cover them first with soft plastic bags (secured loosely at the wrists with rubber bands). In the few instances where you are to use bare hands, you will be specifically instructed to do so.

Rolling with Forearms

When rolling with your forearms, use even, rocking movements and make sure to roll your wrists slightly inward so that you're rolling with the fatty, muscular part of your forearms, not running along the ulna bone, which may cause bruising later on (photos 28 and 29). Keep your fingers relaxed and straight.

Using your Legs

If you choose to use your legs for rolling, find a comfortable chair (perhaps next to a table for support) and place your well tied-off bundle on a rubber entrance mat. Put your feet on top of the bundle and begin rolling (photos 30 and 31). You may perform this method with or without shoes, although heavy walking shoes help apply weight to the work. This method may take some getting used to, but due to the weight of the legs, it produces good shrinking results for items that are not too fragile.

3-D Basics

Creating solid 3-D forms to make buttons, ropes, and closures is another amazing aspect of hand-felted wools. You will feel like a sculptor shaping these forms. Certain scarves in this book have buttons and loops to create closures, or tails for textural design—and one is even made solely from 3-D ropes and beads. Feel free to add some of these features to other scarves and make them uniquely yours.

CHAD'S TECHNIQUES:

BALL BUTTONS

Use for **Lily Pad Wrap** and for the button on the **Boa Boa** neck wrap, if you want one.

Supplies

See individual project for amounts of wool needed

Small container of soapy water (about 1 cup of warm water and enough soap to make the solution soapy)

Towel

Scale

Vinegar or acid rinse (page 20)

Instructions

1 Follow the project instructions and measure out the amount of wool needed for each ball. This ensures that all the balls will be the same size.

2 Divide the wool for each ball into two sections. Take the first section and squish it into a ball shape with your fingers. Dip it into soapy water and squeeze a few times to saturate completely (photo 32).

32

3 Squeeze out the excess water and wrap the remaining section of dry wool around the wet ball (photo 33). Dip it

33

back into the soapy water, remove, and squeeze gently with your fingertips for about two minutes, keeping it in a ball shape.

4 Place the soapy ball in the center of your hands and roll it very gently like you are making a meatball (photo 34). Gradually increase the pressure of your hands as the ball gets firmer. Occasionally dip the ball back into the soapy water, and continue rolling with your hands until it becomes very hard. Rinse by squeezing under hot water, then squeeze several times in a vinegar bath (page 20) to neutralize any leftover soap. Let dry.

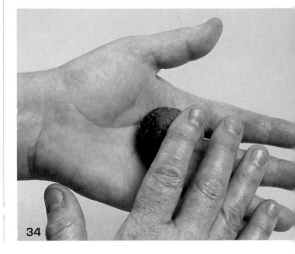

34

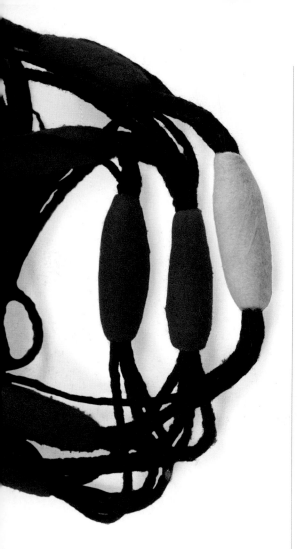

Instructions

1 Divide the wool into 23 sections, for the 23 ball tubes (each weighing .2oz (4g). Use a scale. Note that some ball tubes are yellow and some are red.

2 Take the wool for one ball tube and wrap it tightly around the middle of four pencils, always wrapping in the same direction (photo 35).

3 Dip the wrapped wool ball and pencils in soapy water, and squeeze the wool gently until it is totally saturated (photo 36).

4 Roll the wool/pencil ball gently in one direction between your hands until it starts to hold together (you may need to dip it back into the soapy water),

then roll more vigorously back and forth. The pencils will make a clacking sound (photo 37). Occasionally push the ends of the bead together to keep it from growing too long.

5 When the pencil clacking stops, pull out one pencil and then continue rolling, dipping into the soapy water as needed, until the clacking stops again (photo 38). Remove another pencil. Repeat this process until you are down to one pencil. Continue to roll the one pencil until the bead is very hard.

6 Remove the felt bead and squeeze several times under hot water, then several times in a vinegar rinse to remove all traces of soap (page 20). Reinsert the pencil and roll a few times to make sure the hole stays open. Dry the beads; an easy way is to string all the beads together and hang them in a breeze.

BALL TUBES

Use for **Dread Nauts** These are wonderful tube-like beads ready-made with a large hole for easy stringing onto felted ropes.

Supplies

See project for amounts and colors of wool needed

Scale

Small container of soapy water

4 pencils

Towel

Vinegar rinse

ROPES

Use for Dread Nauts.

Supplies

Wool roving for project

Container of soapy water

Plastic ridged felt mat (two piece),
see Tools on page 13

Sushi mat

Towel

Vinegar rinse

Instructions

TIP: *Set up a production line. It is easier to do the same step to each of the 10 ropes before moving on.*

1 Divide the roving into quarter thickness. You can achieve this by splitting the roving in half lengthwise, and then spilt each in half again. Once that is done, measure and tear the quartered roving into 10 equal ropes, each 96 inches (243.8 cm) long. The ends of shorter roving pieces can be overlapped and then rolled together gently for a minute to make up a 96 inch (243.8 cm) length.

2 With outstretched fingers, very gently roll the whole length of each dry roving on the plastic mat to condense the fibers. The ropes should be round.

3 Gather each rope in your hand and dip it into the soapy water, squeezing several times underwater to make sure the wool is saturated (photo 39). Unfold the ropes carefully and place them on the plastic mat.

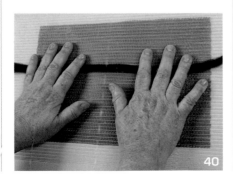

4 Gently roll each rope on the plastic mat with your open hands two times from end to end. Make sure the rope stays round (photo 40).

5 When the rope feels firm, place it between the sushi mat and the plastic mat and roll, pressing hard on the ropes (photo 41). Roll the total length two times.

6 Gather together all 10 ropes and dip them into the soapy water. Squeeze out half the water and toss the ropes hard on the table (page 19) 25 times. Repeat four times (100 tosses total). The ropes should feel very firm. Rinse the ropes vigorously under hot water, then squeeze them in a vinegar rinse (page 20).

7 "Twang" each rope, yanking it hard to straighten and strengthen. Hang to dry.

TAILS

Use for **Blackbeard** Scarf.

Supplies

80 inches (203.2 cm) of roving

Small container of soapy water

Towel

Scale

Vinegar rinse

Instructions

TIP: *Set up a production line. It is easier to perform each step to all 128 tails before moving on.*

1 Divide the black roving down the middle to get two even halves. Then spilt each half again and then once more, so you end up with eight even strips of roving. Tear each of the eight strips into 5-inch (12.7 cm) tails so you have a total of 128 tails. Fold each 5-inch (12.7 cm) tail in half. The folded end will become the tail and the "loose" ends will be the root. Keep the root end dry.

2 Pick up one folded tail and dip the folded half into the soapy water, squeezing a few times to saturate the wool (photo 42). Keep the root ends dry. Squeeze out the excess water.

3 Soft roll: take each wet tail and roll it on a sponge for about a minute until it holds together and is soft but firm (photo 43).

4 Hard roll: dip each tail again in the soapy water (keeping the root end dry) and then roll it against the plastic mat until it is hard. Squeeze out the water in a towel.

5 Opening the root: with dry hands, tear off the excess ragged ends from each tail, leaving about 1 inch (2.5 cm) of dry wool. Open out the dry root wool into a flat circle (photo 44). To attach the tails to your scarf, refer to the project directions.

Jorie's Technique: Cords

Use for **Link Muffler Series** and **Fallen Leaves Collar**

Supplies

Wool roving for project

Bamboo mat

Towel

Felting solution

Instructions

1 To separate the amount needed for each cord, divide and pull away a small section of roving while twisting it. Twist it between the fingers of both hands about 1½ times to check what the thickness will look like after it is felted. Add more or less wool until you find the correct diameter of the strand, then separate the entire length from the main sliver. For the ties for this **Link Muffler Series**, I separated my black roving into eight strands.

2 Run each solid-color strand through your hand under light pressure to check that the entire length of the strand is of even thickness. If you find a lumpy area, pull lengthwise so that the number of fibers will lessen in that zone. If one cord strand is slightly shorter and thicker than the other, gently pull tiny sections at the fattest areas all along the length until the lengths match.

NOTE: *It is easy to break off the fragile strand when you least expect to. If this happens, do not fret. Just overlap the two ends until the thickness equals the rest of the strand, and then gently roll the area back and forth in the palms of your hands. This must be done while the strand is dry.*

3 Place a dampened bamboo mat on top of a towel. Slide a little over an inch (3 cm) of the cord end off the mat, and dry roll the entire length (minus the 1+-inch (3 cm) end) inside the mat for 10 counts per section (photo 45).

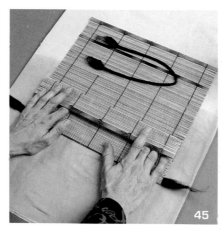

45

4 Once a soft cord form has come to shape, hold the dry end in one hand so it doesn't get wet and sprinkle the wool with hot felting solution. Roll for 20 counts per section. Move to the next section and continue the process until the last 1+ inch (3 cm) end comes into position at the opposite edge of the mat. Leave end dry.

Link Muffler

5 Repeat the rolling process, applying hot felting solution and a little direct soap when necessary until the cord shrinks about 20 percent of its original length. Still keeping the tips dry, rinse the cord well in hot water and then wring out the excess moisture. Stretch out the length and leave it to dry. The finished length is about ⅜ x 35 inches (9.5 mm x 89 cm) including the dry ends.

CHAD'S DYEING BASICS

Several of my scarves in this book require dyeing to achieve their unique beauty. Dyeing needn't be scary or dangerous—just use common sense, think through everything, and pay attention.

My dye kitchen is divided into two areas: the dye mixing area inside my studio, and the actual dyeing area outside on my back porch. My porch is equipped with several hot plates and a propane gas-fed turkey boiler. Outside I have set up several clotheslines and drying racks. I don't dye all the time, just when working on a project. When I need to dye a large quantity of wool— 10 to 20 pounds (4.5 to 9 kg), I'll do it all at once, working with 6 ounces (168 g) at a time. The rest of the time the tools, burners, and dyes are put away and out of harm's way.

DYES, CHEMICALS, AND pH

The dyes I use are both metal complex (Lanasets) and washfast acid dyes. These dyes are for use with protein fibers such as wool and silk, resulting in solid, strong colors. They are available at several dye companies in dozens of colors, but you will only need a few for the projects in this book.

I especially like the metal complex dyes. Most have a tin atom attached to the dye molecule that gives the color a wonderful jewel-like brightness. They have excellent fade resistance and produce the best black dye I have found. Both the acid dyes and the metal complex dyes are prepared and used the same way for the dye pot, which gives you, the dyer, a simpler life.

Acid, in either the dry citric acid form or white vinegar, is used because the dye bath needs to be an acid environment of 4.5 to 5 pH in order for the dye mole-cules to bond with the dye sites on the wool fiber. I like using dry citric acid as it can be stored safely without leaking, has no fumes, and is easily measured with a measuring spoon. You can use vinegar with acid dyes, but citric acid is much cheaper in the long run. It is available from dye supply companies and drugstores.

Checking the pH

You will need to invest in some pH papers (also available from dye companies or a variety of sources) to make sure you have enough acid in the dye bath (photo 46).

46

To check the pH of the water that you will use for dyeing, dip a 1-inch (2.5 cm) piece of the pH paper into the water-filled dye pot. Compare the color of the dipped paper to the color chart on the pH paper case. It is probably around pH 7 (Neutral). To change the pH to the optimum pH of 4.5 to 5 pH, fill a 2-cup (.48 L) glass measuring cup half full of water from the dye pot and add about 1 tablespoon (15 mL) of dry citric acid (or 6 teaspoons [30 mL] of white vinegar). Stir well. Add it all back into the dye pot. Stir. Take the pH measurement of the dye pot again. Has it reached 4.5 to 5pH? If it is still higher than 4.5 to 5, mix and add more acid. If it is lower, add a small bit of baking soda to reduce the acidity. You will only need to figure out once how much acid to add, as all your other dye pots will require the same amount to be added. If you move away or dye with different water, retest the pH again.

The only other chemical used with your dyebath is a water softener, which helps eliminate any metals or chemicals in your water system. Water softeners sequester, or bind with the metals or chemicals that make the water hard and keep them from interfering with the dyeing process. I use about ½ teaspoon (2.5 mL) for each dyebath. This is not necessary if you have soft water or a house water softening system.

Some dyers use a leveling agent in immersion dye baths to help produce even dye color on the wool, but I prefer the wonderful effects and surprises created when the dye attaches to the wool very fast. Sometimes due to the fast take-up abilities of these dyes, the first part of a project placed in the dye pot is a stronger color than the last part.

DYE KITCHENS

It is easiest and safer to have an inside space for mixing the dry powder dyes and chemicals and an outdoor space for using the dye pots. If you do not have specific reserved spaces that can become your dye areas, you'll need to set up temporary ones that can be quickly and easily cleaned when not in use.

For your dye mixing area, refer to photo 47 to see how to make a breeze-proof dye box from a plastic-wrapped cardboard box. Do all your measuring and mixing inside this box, as you do not want dry dye powder blowing about. Place a damp paper towel inside the box to catch stray bits of powder, and be sure to wear your respirator and gloves.

Setting Up a Dye Kitchen

Use this checklist to assemble your dye kitchen:

Location

• A good place for heating dye baths is a protected area outside your house. This can be a fire escape, porch, or deck. Good ventilation is extremely important, and being outside solves that issue. It is also helpful to have a

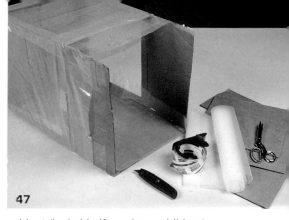

47

cabinet (lockable if you have children) to store your dyes, chemicals, and tools.

Water

• A close source of water is very helpful, even if it is water out of a hose. The less running around carrying hot dye pots, the better.

Just You

• Be the only person (other than a friend who is helping) in your dye area. No children, pets, or interested neighbors. It is essential that you are able to pay full attention to what you are doing to ensure success of your project and the safety of all concerned.

Hot Plates

• Electric hot plates work well for the size of the projects in this book. They are fairly cheap, and can be found in any large housewares department. Single burners are best. Never trust the heat dial, and always unplug when finished with your project. Beware of stringing extension cords about. If they must be in a traffic area, tape them securely to the floor.

Work Surface

• It is best to find a sturdy, low table on which to place the hot plate, as it is better for your back, the dye pot is less likely to be kicked over, and you can see into the pot to know what's happening to your project.

Clothing and Safety

Before starting a dyeing project, consider your clothes. A long waterproof apron that comes to about 4 inches (10.2 cm) below your knees prevents wet clothing and burns if a hot dye bath spills. Heavy rubber gloves are a must for carrying dye pots and taking hot dyed projects out of the pot. Many varieties are available from dye companies and safety stores. Always wear closed-toe shoes—no bare feet or sandals. Hot water is always being dripped or spilled, and your feet are a perfect target.

When finished with a dye bath, the water, which should be clear, can be reused with another dye color. Top off with more water if needed. Add the same amount of acid as before.

Once you are done with the whole dyeing process, if there is still color in the dye bath, it can be saved up to a week. Add more acid as before, toss in some wool roving, and go through the immersion dye bath process. You'll get some great colors and all the dye will be used up. Before dumping out the now clear dye bath, check the pH and add baking soda to raise the pH to neutral (7 pH). Wash all the tools you used and safely store away all the dyes and chemicals.

Good Tools to Have in a Dye Kitchen

The following is a list of the basic essential tools for your dye kitchen. Once used, all tools, especially measuring spoons and cups, can only be used for dyeing. Do not use your kitchen tools.

Several sizes of large (2 to 7 gallon [7.6 to 26.6 L]) rust-free stainless steel pots and lids

Plastic dishpans and 5 gallon (19 L) buckets are also very helpful for holding dyed and undyed projects, and for rinsing and cooling

Electric hot plate (and extension cord if needed)

Low, sturdy dyeing table

Glass measuring cup with handle, 2-cup (.48 L) size

Large stir stick for the dye pot (acrylic is best)

Small metal stir stick for mixing dyes and acid (iced tea spoons work great)

Set of metal measuring spoons

Heavy kitchen-type gloves

Latex gloves (thin ones to keep dye off your hands; available at drugstores)

Dust mask, or even better—a heavy-duty ventilator mask (available from lumber stores and dye companies)

Potholders

Towels

Thermometer (must go up to 212°F [100°C], available from dye companies)

Kitchen timer

Long tongs to remove items from dye bath

Roll of paper towels

Wastepaper bucket lined with plastic bag

RULES OF DYEING

- Be very careful of the dry dye powder. Do not breathe it or get it on any work surfaces or hands. Rinse off measuring spoons and anything covered with wet dye immediately.

- Tightly close all dye containers immediately after use.

- Do not eat or drink in the dye area.

- Do not use any dye tools for eating or other uses. Once in the dye kitchen, always in the dye kitchen.

- Do not use stoves, electric or gas, that are used by anyone for food.

- Clean up as you work. Dripped wet dye will dry and become airborne.

- Do not mix water with electricity.

- Do not allow children or pets in the dye area.

- Use common sense

DYE BATHS FOR RESIST PROJECTS

Immersion Dye Bath

This technique is used to create:

Bubble Boa (variations)

Magic Muffler

Bark Scarf

Immersion dye baths are used when the project needs to be all one color. Set up your dye kitchen.

Instructions

1 Fill dye pot three-quarters full of lukewarm water and place on electric hot plate. Turn on heat. Cover with lid. Set the timer for 15 minutes.

2 Using the glass measuring cup, remove 2 cups (.48 L) of water from the dye pot, and add enough citric acid or vinegar to raise the pH of the dye pot to 4.5 to 5 pH (see instructions on page 31). Add to dye bath.

3 Take out another cup (.24 L) of water from the dye bath, and add about ½ teaspoons of dye powder (add twice as much when dyeing black) (photo 48). Stir very well and pour into the dye bath. Stir.

4 Take the temperature of the dye bath. When it reaches 175°F (80° C), (photo 49) put your project in and stir gently. Set your timer for 45 minutes.

5 Keep the dye bath at 175 to 200°F (80 to 93°C) for 45 minutes. Check every 10 minutes to make sure it doesn't boil.

6 When the time is up, turn off the hot plate and unplug the cord. Use hot pads and the tongs to remove your dyed project, and place it in a bucket (photo 51).

7 Run cold water over the project until it is cool enough to touch. Take off any clamps, plastic, and papers used (photo 52). Rinse the project until the water runs clear.

8 Check the individual project instructions for drying instructions.

Hot Water Bath for Thermal Shaping

This technique is used to create:

Bubble Boa

Bark Scarf variations

This simple method is just the dye bath above without any dye. Follow the time and temperature directions. Follow individual project instructions for rinsing scarf.

Dry Dye Powder Dyeing

This technique is used to create the lovely watercolor effects for:

Classic Airy Fairy Scarf

Inge's Fancy

Lily Pad Wrap

Dry powder dyeing is as it sounds. The loose wool roving is saturated in a small amount of clear dye bath (just water and the citric acid), and then various colors of dry dye powders are carefully sprinkled on top of the wet

wool. During the heating process, the colors mix and produce beautiful results. The trick to not felting the roving together during the dyeing process is to NEVER STIR the roving once it is heating and NEVER BOIL THE DYE POT. This technique can be done working with children, using different flavors/colors of non-sweetened soft drink mixes as they dye. The directions for using the acid/metal complex dyes or the soft drink mix "dyes" are the same. Just be extremely careful with the real dyes.

Additional Supplies Needed

Dry Merino roving, up to 6 ounces (168 g), torn into 1-ounce (28 g) lengths for ease of handling. See the project supply lists for amounts.

3 or 4 different colors of washfast acid dyes and/or metal complex dyes (or packages of soft drink flavors)

Instructions

1 Fill a small dye pot one-quarter full of cool water.

2 Add enough citric acid or vinegar to bring the pH to 4.5-5 pH. Stir well (step 2, page 33).

3 Add the dry Merino roving to the acid bath. Gently push down the roving until it is saturated (photo 53).

4 Put on a mask and gloves. Arrange all dyes and individual measuring spoons near the dye pot. Carefully and slowly open one jar, take out about ½ to ¼ teaspoon (.5 to 1 g) of dry powder, and securely close the lid. Place your hand about 1 inch (2.5 cm) from the surface of the wet wool and gently tap the spoon, spreading the dye powder in different areas (photo 54). Rinse the spoon immediately. Continue in like fashion with up to but no more than three other colors (or it gets muddy).

5 Gently poke the dry clumps of dye on the surface of the wet wool with the stir stick to help them dissolve (photo 55). Slowly poke any white wool areas under the surface of the dye bath.

6 Slide the stir stick between the side of the pot and the wet wool, and

slowly push the wool toward the center (photo 56). Do this all around the pot. This helps the dye bath reach all areas of the wool. Do not poke a lot or the color will get muddy. Do not stir or poke after this step.

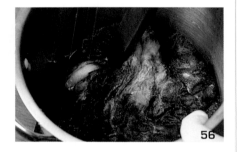

7 Place the dye pot on the hot plate and raise the temperature to JUST 175°F (80°C). Set your timer for 45 minutes. Check every 10 minutes to make sure the temperature stays between 175 and 200°F (80 and 93°C). Do not boil.

8 When the time is up, slide the dyed wool and remaining dye bath out of the dye pot into a plastic dish tub (this will feel just like an oyster). Let it sit until it is cool to the touch.

9 Gently press out excess water from each piece of roving and hang on a line to dry.

10 When almost dry, I shake the rovings individually to toss water off the tips and to puff out the wool. This makes it much easier to divide later when you are laying out a scarf.

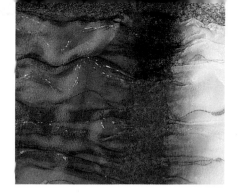

JORIE'S INSTRUCTIONS FOR DYEING SILK FABRIC

This technique is used to create:
Dip Dyed Party Scarf

You can dye silk fiber and fabric using the same procedure and dye product as when dyeing wool fibers with acid dye. The same principals apply but the recommended maximum temperature of the dye bath is 175°F (80°C). Too high of a temperature will weaken the silk and may damage the fibers enough to take the sheen away.

Instructions

1 Before wetting your fabric for dyeing, fold it into thirds or fourths so the width will be narrower than the diameter of your dye pot.

2 Baste a thick rayon or polyester thread across the area to be dyed, as once the fabric has been lowered into the dye pot it is easy to lose track of the exact area you wish to dye.

3 If you want a fairly straight line, roll the fabric onto a wooden dowel (cover the dowel first with plastic wrap to avoid staining the fabric) or stainless pipe, and secure it with clean clips. Take precautions to cover the white portion with a plastic bag, as just one little "blip" of dye will stain the fabric instantly. As you can see in the photo on page 94 of the **Dip Dyed Party Scarf**, one third of the fabric was left the original white.

4 Lower the fabric into the dye pot until the basted line stops just at the bath level, adjusting the rolled length if necessary or add more hot water to raise the dye bath levels. Expect the dye to travel up the fabric a bit. Rest the free ends of the rod on the top of the pot (photo 57) until the desired color is achieved. Occasionally swirl the dye around in the pot, and remove the fabric to check the intensity of the color.

5 When the desired depth of color is reached, carefully lift out the fabric, rinse well, and hang to dry.

6 Dispose of the dye bath responsibly (page 32).

Hand Carding Practice and Color Sampling

To enhance your personal color palette and to save time rather than ordering or dyeing a new color, consider fiber blending using hand carders. Unique custom colors can be created by hand carding because unlike watercolors or oils, which, when mixed well, become one color, fibers blend, producing interesting colors with added depth. Fiber blending allows you the flexibility to prepare colors that are strikingly brilliant, or ones that are subtly graduated in hue. You can also use hand carders to mix in other fibers with the wool, like silk or flax. For a truly special item, you can even blend good felting wool with the fine undercoat from your own pet.

This technique is used in the Fallen Leaves Collar.

Choose a pair of whatever colors you think you'd like to see turned into a muffler. Consider complementary colors like orange and turquoise, or bright pink and medium gray. Learning proper carding techniques takes practice, so be patient.

Supplies

2.5 g of wool in each of two different colors

Scale

Pair of hand carders (you can substitute a pair of soft wire-toothed pet brushes)

5 Once the wool has been transferred to the opposite carder, simply switch the hand carders around from one hand to the other.

6 Continue, moving through the marbled stage until the blend is even in color (photo 60). Lift the small batt off the carder and set aside; start again with the next batch of two colors. After completing all five batches, check them for general color evenness. If one batch is off, blend that one with another and the overall effect will even out.

Instructions

1 Weigh out 2.5 g of each color. Eyeball and separate each color into five parts, each weighing 0.5 g (photo on page 36). Mix a pair of colors together with your fingers to expedite the start of the blending process.

2 Hook a batch of mixed fibers onto the teeth of one of the two hand carders, using the weight of your palm to force the fibers into place (photo 58).

58

3 Place the carder with the fibers in the palm of your left hand and find the best balance point near where the handle and carder are joined. Tightly grip the other carder in your right hand, teeth down, and using an arcing motion, pass it gently over the teeth and wool of the left carder. The handles should be facing in opposite directions,

and you should be pulling them away from each other.

4 Begin at the base of the left carder, and as if you were combing your own hair, gently hook and stroke the surface of the left carder with the right carder, ending with an upward pulling motion. With each subsequent stroke, move up another inch (2.5 cm) higher on the left carder, hooking with the right carder some of the wool from the left. Within five or six strokes the fibers should be transferred from the left carder to the right (photo 59).

59

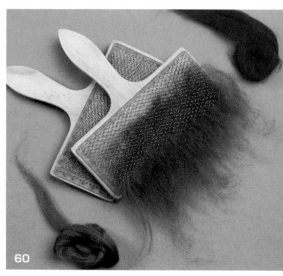

60

NOTE: *The fibers will continue to blend during the felting process, so within five or six changes of the hand carder you should reach a suitable result.*

Depending on the surface area of your carders, you should not try to blend more than about 3 g at a time. If you can't see or feel the teeth, there is too much wool and you are losing time trying to work that much even if it appears like a tiny amount. Take your time and beware of the enthusiast beginner's "tennis" elbow!

FLAT BRAID SAMPLING

You'll use this technique when creating the **Father's Day Muffler** and the **Wedding Stole**. This process is considered braiding because each consecutive lengthwise strand (or warp strand) becomes the cross filler (or weft), similar to a three-strand braid used in everyday hairstyles. In weaving, as in basketry, the lengthwise (warp) and crosswise (weft) threads are discontinuous. The three techniques share the same basic structure where one strand runs, systematically, over one thread and under the next. In weaving, this is called a "basic" or "plain" weave; it is referred to as "plaiting" in basketry; and for multiple-strand flat braiding, where the resulting fabric is the same except produced on a diagonal, it is known as a "bias" weave.

Before you attempt either the Father's Day Muffler or the Wedding Stole, follow the instructions below and make a practice sample.

Practice Sample Supplies
60-inch (152.4 cm) length of roving of any wool such as 64 Merino, 58 crossbred, Romney, or Corriedale in three colors

NOTE: *This technique was developed for use with long staple breeds like Romney, that are commonly used for spinning. It gives an added substructure to an otherwise spongier felt.*

PRACTICE SAMPLE INSTRUCTIONS

1 Subdivide the roving to prepare narrower strands for braiding. The average rope-like roving is far too thick in the state it comes in, so it must be carefully separated to a narrower width. To do this, separate the roving lengthwise to make two halves, then divide those halves into half again, and finally, separate each half into thirds. Thus at least 12 strands can be separated from the roving. In image 61, you see the original ball of white roving, and the subsequent divisions of ½ strand, ¼ strand, and three ¹⁄₁₂ strands in a row.

61

Practice with a short length of commonly available roving, as each manufacturer's quality will be slightly different in bulk fatness. You may also find that some roving is easily divisible into even width strands, while others prove more difficult. You want to achieve as evenly separated roving strands as possible. It is a matter of preference and skill as to how thin you prefer your strands.

2 Next, under minimal pressure, gently slide each strand through one closed fist to check if each is of even thickness. If you feel a bump, or in general the entire strand feels fatter, then most likely there are more wool fibers in this area. If this is the case, gently pull at the spot to lessen the amount of wool, which in turn will elongate the strand by some millimeters. Be careful not to break the strand in two—after you do this once you will know exactly what I mean!

3 Before starting to braid, spread open the width of each strand down its entire length. You want to create a lightweight fabric, and therefore need to spread out each strand to about a 1-inch (2.5 cm) width, as shown in photo 62. Photo 63 illustrates how you should be able to see the tabletop through the strand. If the strand still appears too thick or too wide after being spread open, you have started with too thick of a strand, so subdivide it again.

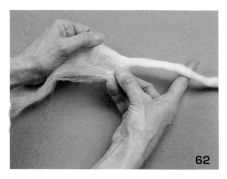
62

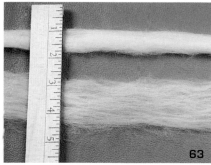
63

4 For ease in instruction, start the sample with the correct color sequence as seen in the sample (photo 64). Use a wide, heavy, and smooth

object, such as a phone book, as a weight, and place it across the strands, one-quarter distance from the far end.

64

5 You'll find it easier to begin from the center, rather than the side, with the white strands crossing over (page 40, photos A–C) or under each strand. Once the four white strands are set in place, try to hook the next cross strand under the lifted strands. No cheating—you will find it easier if you lift the entire strand up and rest it on the weight before positioning the next consecutive cross strand. Continue with the yellow section (photos D–I), and finish in succession with the four blue strands (photos J–M).

6 Now you are ready to start another white round. This time begin from the outside left strand. From this point on, it is important to curve each strand around corners rather than fold it over on top of itself. Once the white round has been completed, continue with the next four yellow strands, and so on in the same progression.

NOTE: *Each braided strand stops to the left or right of center and NEVER crosses over to the far edge.*

7 Due to the interlacing of the strands, you will notice that once a couple of full sequences have been

BRAIDING STEPS

A

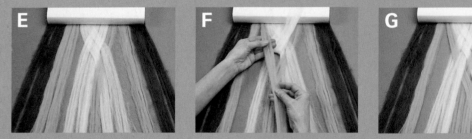

B

C

D

E

F

G

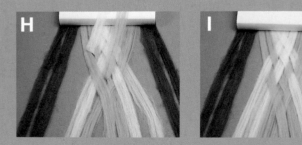

H

I

J

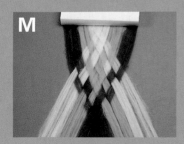

K

L

M

braided, the initial width has narrowed to about two-thirds of the original (photo 65). Mark the desired width on the weight to maintain the same size throughout the braiding process. For the sample, an 8-inch (20.5 cm) width was maintained. This braid width is still expected to shrink 18 to 20 percent smaller once felted.

65

You can now calculate that 12 strands of 1-inch (2.5 cm) width will produce a felted fabric with a finished width of about 6½ inch (16.5 cm). You can either start with more or less strands, wider or narrower strands, or, as in the case of the Wedding Stole project, make more than one braided band and stitch them together before the felting begins. This is a wonderful technique for blankets, as well as garments like vests and ponchos.

Follow the "over one strand and under the next strand" movement, and soon it will become second nature to braid a wide bias fabric. **Caution:** Do not try to speed through the process by slipping the strands through semi-raised warps. Lift up and place the warp on top of the weight before sending the cross strands through.

8 When the strand length has just about run out, you are finished braiding the first half. Now remove the weight, turn over the sample and flip it around, replace the weight, and braid from the center to the other end. Before starting the second half, check the angles of the diagonal cross-strands and tighten the center area that was under the weight. From this point on, continuing the braid is easier than the start. Just begin braiding either of the outermost strands, working from the side that has the most strands. Alternating sides, work the braid until you have once again run out of length.

9 To square off the end of the braid sample, (photo 66), continue braiding, but stop one less cross-strand from the center sooner each time, until the last outer strand crosses under or over only one strand. Stabilize the ends of the dry braid before felting by basting a thick thread across the bottom and then back again, making sure to tie off the thread (photo 67). Repeat squaring off and stitching the opposite unfinished end.

66

67

10 Cut off or even up the straggly ends. For felting the sample, follow the directions for **Father's Day Braided Muffler** on page 104. Photo

68

68 shows a "before" and "after" sanded sample, demonstrating how the vibration from the sander advances the felting process by stabilizing the diagonal fibers (before the rougher rolling process begins). Photo 69 illustrates the widthwise shrinking of the sample through use of hot felting solution and soft plastic bags over the hands.

69

NOTE: *Once felted, the length of sample fabric can be cut in two and then stitched into a couple of pouches, so you will not find the time invested in practicing wasted in any way.*

You are working with rather short strands here, but will graduate to longer strands for the two projects that follow. You will also learn how to add on or change color when a strand length runs out, making it possible to vary the design image. Once the strand is woven, it can be felted like the **Father's Day Braided Muffler** (page 104), or stitched together with a blind reinforcing stitch and then felted into a shawl, like the **Wedding Stole** found on page 117.

CHAD ALICE HAGEN

MAJOR MOMENTS IN A PERSONAL TEXTILE HISTORY

Sitting under the dining room table, trying to mimic my mother's knitting with my own dirty bit of string and two stubby pencils. Didn't work very well.

While taking a break from picking apples, I wander into the weaving room at Evergreen college—all those threads! Discovered that I could get an actual degree in textiles at University of Wisconsin: became a student.

A student demonstration in Our Friends the Fibers class turned the exotic word "feltmaking" into a real world of pinning wool fleece between sheets and stamping the package while showering. Felting was beautiful and a miracle.

The shower stomp, kool-aid dyes, and gifts of dirty fleece from aging sheep just aren't pretty anymore. A workshop with Layne Goldsmith at Arrowmont School of Arts and Crafts (Tennessee) teaches me traditional felting with reed mats and

successful dyeing with real dyes. Goodbye to
happy hands at home experimentation. Got a
BA in Art and an MS in textile history. Became
a career rag rug weaver.

Attend Cranbrook Academy of Art (MFA '88) working with
my beloved wool; exploring the *art* of feltmaking. Make
huge, labor-intensive felt works composed of thousands
of individually felted shapes hand stitched together and
refelted. Started teaching feltmaking and entered shows.
Became a real artist in a loft in Minnesota.

Awarded a Fulbright Cultural Award to teach feltmaking in
New Zealand. Met Merino wool and said hello to resist
dyeing. Moved to endless study of surface design of the
felt textile; the burnt, dyed, over-dyed, resist dyed, rubbed,
stitched, cut, beaded, and glued surface of felt.

Moved to Asheville, North Carolina, and realized I had
come home. Started writing felt books for Lark. Continue
to teach full time, hang out in the studio full time, write full
time, garden full-time, clean house
full time, and be an artist.

chadhagen

**A student demonstration
in Our Friends the Fibers
class turned the exotic
word "feltmaking" into a
real world of pinning
wool fleece between
sheets and stamping the
package while shower-
ing. Felting was beautiful
and a miracle.**

AIRY
FAIRY
SCARF

THIS SCARF IS A CLASSIC OF FELT-MAKING. I HAVE EXPERIMENTED WITH DIFFERENT IDEAS FOR YEARS, CONSTANTLY CHANGING THE DIRECTIONS TO INCLUDE SIMPLIFIED LAYOUTS, DIFFERENT FELTING TECHNIQUES, AND EXPERIMENTAL SHAPES. WRAPPED A FEW TIMES AROUND YOUR NECK, IT IS A WARM—AND STUNNING—SCARF THAT ALSO LOCKS FABULOUS WHEN MADE SMALLER AND TIED AROUND YOUR HEAD. MADE LARGER, IT BECOMES A STRIKING SHAWL. IT IS STILL ONE OF MY FAVORITE SCARVES TO MAKE AND TO WEAR.

Supplies

2 to 2.5 oz Merino wool (fine wool or 64 tops)

Felting kit (page 12)

Two wooden ice cream sticks (or your fingers)

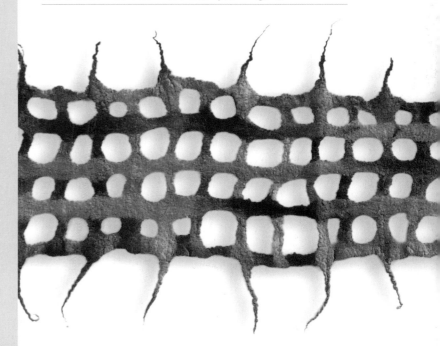

Instructions

1 Follow step 1 on page 17, and draw a 96 x 9-inch (243.8 x 22.9 cm) layout pattern.

2 Divide your wool into three equal sections. Take the first section of roving and divide it into workable sections. Lay out three horizontal rows, each 1 inch (2.5 cm) apart from the other in the center of your layout area. Pull out the wool in thin strips as shown (photo 1). You may have some wool left over; if so just put it aside.

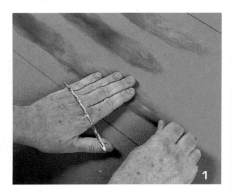

3 Using the second section of wool, lay out the vertical rows, also about 1 inch (2.5 cm) apart. Extend the rows approximately 2 inches (5 cm) beyond the drawn pattern lines (photo 2). If you run out of wool, use leftovers from the first section.

4 Using the third section of wool, lay one horizontal row on both sides of the center rows, going over the vertical rows as shown in photo 3.

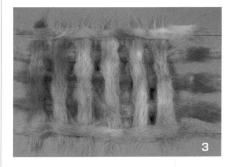

Fringe

5 For each vertical row that you don't want to be fringed, fold over the top and bottom wool that extends beyond the last horizontal row. Where you DO want fringe, lay an additional shingle of wool on top of the wool that extends beyond the last horizontal rows (photo 4). Don't forget fringe at the ends of the scarf.

6 Wet and felt the scarf using the directions on page 18 (steps 9 through 12) (photo 5).

7 Do three stones of Sharpei rub. Use two ice cream sticks or your fingers to open up all the spaces between the horizontal and vertical rows (photo 6). Continue with two more Sharpei rubs and then step 13 (page 19) to finish.

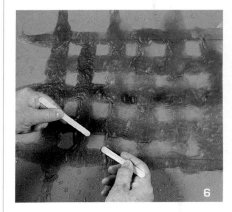

8 Lay scarf flat on a clean table and stretch it back into a rectangle. You may want to gently tear open any closed or small holes, and trim any "spiderwebs" that may be in the hole areas (photo 7). Let dry and then iron.

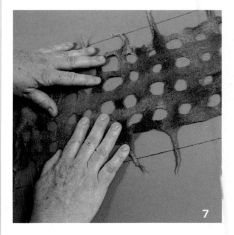

MR. SATURDAY NIGHT

HERE IS A HANDSOME SCARF

MADE IN TWO PARTS—DOUBLE THE STYLE AND DOUBLE THE NATURAL COLORS—THANKS TO ALPACA FIBER. HUACAYA ALPACA IS VERY SOFT AND BECAUSE IT DOESN'T HAVE THE CRIMP OR CURL OF WOOL, FEELS DIFFERENT FROM THE SHEEP WOOLS. SINCE IT HAS NO SCALES ON THE FIBER SHAFT IT WILL BE SLIPPERY TAKING A BIT LONGER TO FELT. THIS SCARF IS AN EXCELLENT EXCUSE TO SPLURGE ON SOME GREAT DECORATIVE BUTTONS, OR CHECK YOUR TREASURE BOX FOR ONES THAT YOU'VE BEEN SAVING FOR SOMETHING SPECIAL.

SUPPLIES

2.5 to 3.0 oz (70 to 84 g) light gray Huacaya alpaca fiber (in roving form)

2.0 to 2.5 oz (56 to 70 g) dark gray Huacaya alpaca fiber (in roving form)

Felting kit (page 12)

Two-part plastic felt mat

Tweezers

4 fabulous buttons

Buttonhole thread and needle

NOTE: *You will be making each scarf separately and then joining them together with buttons.*

INSTRUCTIONS

1 Draw a layout pattern of 10 x 96 inches (25.4 x 243.8 cm). Start with the light gray scarf and, following steps 1 through 8 on page 17 divide the fiber into three equal sections (one for each of three layers) and lay it out. Notice when you lay out the alpaca fiber, it is very lofty. Be sure to lay out even amounts of the fiber and take extra time "patting the bunny" (page 16, step 4) and dry felting (page 17, step 8).

2 Follow steps 9 through 13 (page 18) and continue felting the light gray scarf. You'll notice that when you sprinkle on the soapy water in step 9, the fiber will flatten down considerably (photo 1).

3 When you reach step 13—after the sharpei rub, the fiber will still need more felting. Place a scarf on the two-part plastic felting mat and rub it up and down on the plastic mat for two stones (page 13), using the damp sponges to help move the scarf (photo 2). Finish felting following steps 13 through 22 on pages 19–20. Stretch the scarf back into a rectangular shape and dry flat.

4 To make the dark gray scarf, draw a layout pattern of 8 x 96 inches (20.3 x 243.8 cm). Divide the fiber, lay it out, and then felt it the same way as you did the light gray scarf.

5 Pass a damp sponge over each finished dry scarf to pull off loose fibers. Use the tweezers to pull out any vegetable matter still left in the scarves (photo 3).

6 Arrange the smaller scarf on top of the larger. Place one button near each end of the scarf, and two others equidistant from the center. Sew on with buttonhole thread, stitching through both scarves (photo 4).

Llamas, and both suri and hucaya (wa-ca-ya) alpacas all produce attractive fibers that can be spun and made into incredibly soft fabrics. Since alpaca is

lanolin-free and lacks a cuticle there is an added bonus in that it is naturally hypoallergenic. I like using huacaya alpaca as it felts so nicely. Treat yourself and try felting some of these fibers for a new hands-on experience. This scarf will shed a bit after felting so wear it with those nice heathery grays.

BOA BOA

ARE ONE OF THE MOST BEAUTIFUL FEATURES OF WOOL. I HAVE BAGS OF WOOL FROM DIFFERENT BREEDS STACKED TO THE RAFTERS IN MY STUDIO, JUST TO LOOK AT. THIS SCARF/MUFFLER USES LOCKS OF MOHAIR AS ITS FOCAL POINT, AND IT FEELS WONDERFULLY SINFUL TO WRAP THE SOFT CURLY LOCKS AROUND YOUR NECK. YOU MAY ALSO MAKE IT SHORTER, ADD A BUTTON AND LOOP, AND HAVE A NECK WARMER.

SUPPLIES

.75 oz (21 g) Merino roving, in your choice of color (washed or unwashed)

1 oz (28 g) curly wool locks

Felting kit (page 12)

NOTE: *Be sure to choose a soft fleece like mohair or blue faced Leicester, as large diameter fleeces will poke and irritate your bare neck. Also try dyeing the locks using the directions on page 34 (dry dye powder).*

Lincoln, blue faced Leicester, and Mohair locks

INSTRUCTIONS

1 Refer to page step 1 on page 17 and draw a 8 x 72-inch (20.36 x 182.9 cm) layout pattern.

2 Divide the Merino roving into two sections and lay out two layers. Then, following steps 2 through 13 on pages 17–19, felt to the prefelt stage. Gently squeeze out as much water as possible. Lay the prefelt out on your table and straighten. Be careful, as the prefelt is very fragile at this stage and can stretch.

3 Cut the prefelt in half lengthwise as shown in photo 1.

4 Fold each prefelt in half several times lengthwise and trim the uncut side as shown in photo 2.

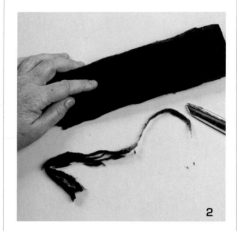

5 Lay down one piece of prefelt. Pick apart the wool locks to separate those that look good and curly. Note the difference between the root end and the curly tip. Tease out the root ends and lay them at the center of the prefelt as shown in photo 3. Continue all the way around. When you are finished, spray the center prefelt with soapy water to help the locks stay in place.

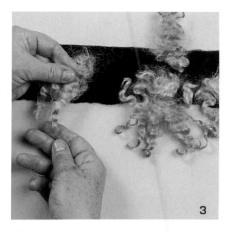

6 Place the second piece of prefelt down on top of the arranged locks and wet it with soapy water (photo 4). Don't rub the outside locks or get them wet. Gently pat the center until it's saturated (step 10, page 18). This scarf takes a bit more care because the raw wool locks have dirt and lanolin on them and will need more soap. Add more soap by rubbing the bar of soap with your hands and then gently rubbing the prefelt. The locks will get wet and cleaned as you work the prefelt.

7 The locks will make the prefelts slide around at first. Check that you are not moving the prefelts off the locks. Before you continue to felt the scarf (following steps 12 through 22 on pages 18–20), make sure both sides have felted together by pinching the prefelt and seeing if the locks have felted to it. When the scarf is fully felted, you will see cut ends of the locks coming through the center of the felt.

8 Lay the scarf flat on the table to dry, gently separating any tangled locks (photo 5), and stretching and shaping the center felt. Let dry.

5

BARK SCARF

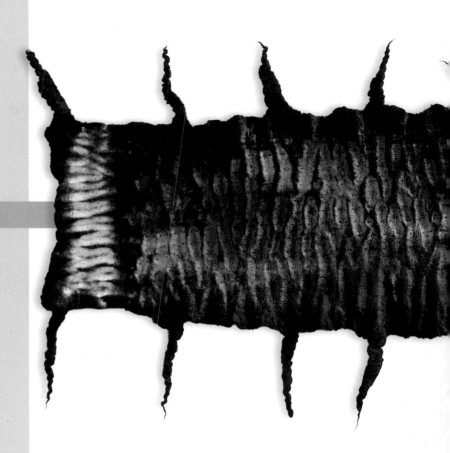

IN JAPAN, THIS SHIBORI STITCHING TECHNIQUE IS USED ON SILK AND COTTON TO PRODUCE A WONDERFUL PATTERN CALLED WOOD GRAIN, OR MOKUME. WHEN THE TECHNIQUE IS USED ON WOOL WHICH IS THEN PROCESSED IN A HOT WATER BATH, THE SAME PATTERN EMERGES WITH AN ADDITIONAL BONUS: THERMAL SHAPING. SO NOT ONLY DOES THE PATTERN LOOK LIKE TREE BARK, IT ALSO HAS TEXTURAL RIDGES TO SUGGEST THE TREES.

SUPPLIES

2 to 2.5 oz Merino roving, 24 micron, in a light color
Strong white string*

Big-eyed sharp-pointed needle

Small curved manicure scissors (optional)

Felting kit (page 12)

Immersion dye bath in dark color (page 33)

Adhesive bandages (several to place on fingers when pulling string tight)

NOTE: *The string needs to be very strong when wet, so soak a sample of your string for 10 minutes and then try to break it. The string should resist breaking. If it breaks, don't use it and find something else.*

Instructions

1 Divide the wool roving into three sections and lay out using a 10 x 96-inch (25.4 x 243.8 cm) layout pattern (page 17, steps 1 through 8).

2 Felt the scarf following steps 9 through 22 on pages 18–20. When finished, stretch the scarf back into a rectangle and dry flat.

Stitching

Thread your needle with a 5-foot (1.5 m) length of heavy string. Do not knot the ends. You will be stitching with a single thread. Use a running stitch, in and out, varying the length of the stitches and the placement of the stitches in the row. Do not try to make the stitches match, as you want an irregular stitch to create interesting shapes (no smocking).

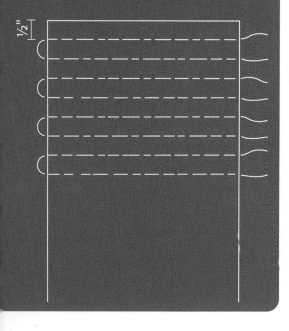

3 Starting at one end of the scarf, stitch a line straight across the scarf. Then loop the string out about 1 inch (2.5 cm) and stitch another line roughly ½ inch (1.3 cm) below the first row back to the starting edge (photo 1). Leave approximately 3 inches (7.6 cm) of thread and then cut. Do this **double-line** stitching every 6 inches (15.2 cm) along the scarf. These pairs of stitched "marker rows" will help you keep your other stitched rows straight.

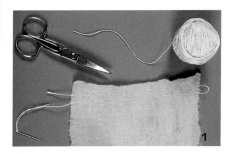

4 Start to fill in the areas between the marker rows with more of the same double rows of stitches, each ½ inch (1.3 cm) from each other. Make sure you cut your thread after every double row. You should have all the string loops on one side, and the cut strings on the other side (photo 2).

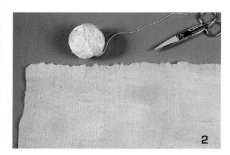

5 IMPORTANT: After all the stitching has been completed, you are ready to pull the stitches tight and dye the scarf. Soak it for at least 20 minutes in warm water, squeezing until it is completely saturated.

6 Place your hand over the wet rows of stitches as shown, and pull each thread so half the stitches are half gathered together all along the length of the scarf (photo 3). Then go back to the beginning and tighten the stitches all the way. The stitches need to be pulled VERY tight, hence the need for very strong string and bandages.

7 After pulling and tightening the stitches, tie each pair of threads with a sturgeon's knot (like a granny knot only wrap the string twice). Finish with a double knot. Snip off the excess strings 2 inches (5 cm) from the knots (photo 4).

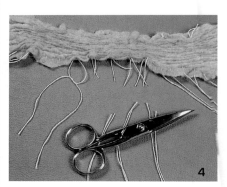

8 Prepare the immersion dye bath with a dark contrasting dye color (page 33). Place the prepared scarf in the water at the correct temperature and set your timer. When finished, take the scarf out of the dye pot with tongs and place into a bucket of cold water.

9 I like to cut the stitches before drying the scarf so that it opens up more and dries faster. To do this, carefully snip off just the knots (curved manicure scissors work best for this). When all the knots are removed, spread open the folds as wide as you wish (photo 5). Remove the remaining threads once the scarf is completely dry.

VARIATIONS

There are many ways to change the appearance of this scarf. One is to cut and remove all the thread while the scarf is wet, and iron flat with a hot steam iron.

Clear dye bath variation: make the scarf in a color of your choice. Stitch and gather the scarf following the directions on the facing page, and then use a clear dye bath (page 34) to set the stitches without adding any further color.

5

BLACKBEARD

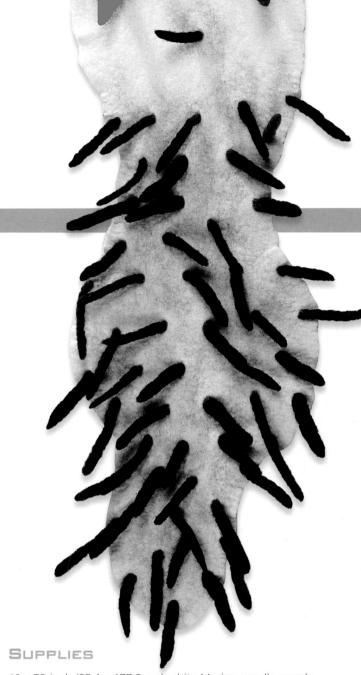

THIS DRAMATIC SCARF MAKES USE

OF MERINO NEEDLE FELTS—A WOOL

PRODUCT RECENTLY ADAPTED FROM

INDUSTRY FOR THE HOME FELTER.

DEPENDING ON THE COLORS CHO-

SEN FOR THE TAILS AND THE BACK-

GROUND, YOU CAN DRAMATICALLY

CHANGE THE SCARF'S LOOK. I DON'T

KNOW WHICH IS MORE FUN—MAKING

OR WEARING THIS SCARF.

SUPPLIES

10 x 70-inch (25.4 x 177.8 cm) white Merino needle punch batt, medium-weight

80-inch (203.2 cm) black Merino roving

Plastic felt mat

Layout pattern (page 61)

Plastic sheeting

Felting kit (page 12)

Craft knife

NEEDLE FELT

Needle felts (also called prefelts) are commercially produced by laying carded wool fleece on large beds where thousands of barbed needles on the top and bottom stab and intermingle the fibers until a sturdy, coherent wool batt results. Using needle felts eliminates the wool layout and dry felting processes, but the needle felt still needs to be fully felted. They are just another way to work with the wool. Needle felt batts come in different weights and wools. In this project you will be using a medium to heavyweight batt.

NOTE: *The individual parts of this scarf are made first, and then assembled and felted. Hard felt the tails beforehand, so they will not attach to the prefelt batt when you are felting.*

INSTRUCTIONS

1 Follow the directions on page 28 (steps 1 to 5), and divide up the black wool roving to make 128 black tails.

2 Because the needle felt will shrink while wet felting, make the pattern 15–20% larger than your final design. Enlarge the layout pattern, cut it out, and place it on top of the Merino needle felt. Trace the outline with a marker, and cut out (photo 1).

3 Lay the cut needle felt out flat on the worktable. Place 50 tails at either end of the scarf. Set aside the remaining 28 tails until later. Working from the front of the scarf, poke the craft knife blade through the needle felt and insert a tail from underneath, pulling the felted part through to the top side (photo 2). Evenly space the tails over the bottom 25 inches of each end of the scarf. DO NOT make holes any closer than ½ inch (1.3 cm) from the edge.

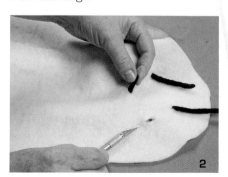

4 When you have finished inserting 50 tails on both scarf ends, evenly scatter and insert the 28 reserved tails over the middle portion of the scarf (photo 3).

5 Turn the scarf over and carefully fluff out the root ends into circles (photo 44 on page 28). Keep about ½ inch (1.3 cm) clear around all the edges. Try to cover the back of the scarf as shown in photo 4. Turn the scarf back over.

6 Wet felt the scarf according to the directions on pages 18–20 (steps 9 to 22). When finished, squeeze scarf in a towel to remove as much water as possible. Lay it flat on the table, and straighten the edges back into the pattern shape.

7 Pull and rub each tail to straighten and shape it (photo 5). Let dry flat.

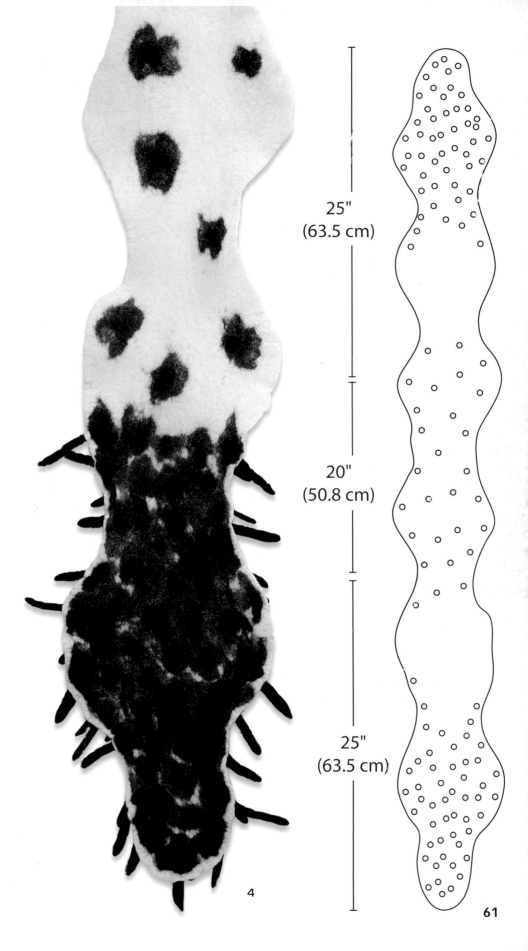

25"
(63.5 cm)

20"
(50.8 cm)

25"
(63.5 cm)

INGE'S FANCY

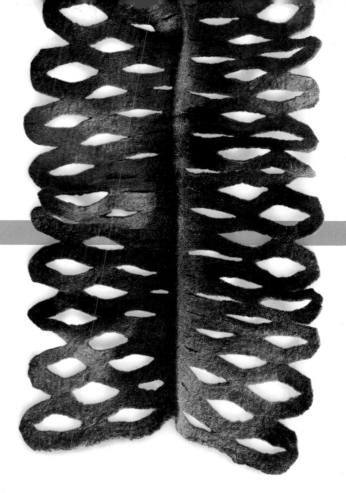

THE BEAUTY OF INGE'S FANCY STARTS WITH THE WATERCOLOR EFFECTS PRODUCED BY THE DRY DYE POWDER DYEING OF THE ROVING. THE RESULTING COLOR VARIATIONS ARE SO ATTRACTIVE THAT YOU COULD WEAR THIS SCARF WITHOUT ANY CUTTING OR BLOCKING. BUT CAREFUL SNIPPING AND STRETCHING COMPLETELY CHANGE THE SURFACE INTO DELICATE, LACY WAVES WHEN THIS SCARF IS WORN OPEN. ANOTHER FASCINATING RESULT OF THE CUTTING AND STITCHING TECHNIQUE IS THAT WHEN THIS SCARF IS FOLDED IN HALF, IT MAKES A FABULOUS SCALLOPED LACE COLLAR THAT COULD BE SECURED WITH A FEW STITCHES OR BUTTONS TO HOLD THE SHAPE.

SUPPLIES

2 to 2.5 oz (56 to 70 g) Merino, 17 or 24 micron, dry dye powder-dyed

Felting kit (page 12)

Very sharp small-bladed scissors for cutting

White or contrasting sewing thread and needle

12-inch-square (30.5 cm) piece of scrap fabric for practice cuts

FYI: *One of the fascinating properties of hand-felted wool is that you can cut into it without any of the raveling or instability that would come with other textile fabrics. I call this scarf Inge's Fancy because I started experimenting with cutting to make the lacy effect and scallops while teaching at the studio of wonderful German felter, Inge Bauer.*

CUTTING PATTERN

Paper pattern, practice pattern, and a cut scarf.

CUTTING NOTES

To help stretch open each cut, cut the scarf while it is damp. It helps to roll up the part of the scarf on which you are not working, and place that end in a plastic bag to keep it damp. Practice the cutting layout on a piece of scrap cloth first. You may want to measure and draw lines on the practice fabric to help you with the first few cuts, but once you get going, use just your eyes and occasionally measure to estimate the distance between the rows of cuts and the lengths of the cuts themselves. Remember, each cut is 3/8 inch (9.5 mm), and the distance between cuts and each row of cutting is 3/8 inch (9.5 mm). Also, note how every other row in the cutting layout starts by cutting into the outside edge of the scarf. That row has three cuts and the alternate rows have two cuts. When you round off the corners of the outside edge cuts, you create a beautiful lacy scallop.

INSTRUCTIONS

1 Dye the roving according to the dry dye powder directions on page 34.

2 Draw a 9 x 72-inch (22.9 x 182.9 cm) layout pattern on your workspace. This scarf tends to stretch after being cut, so the final length will be more like 96 inches (243.8 cm).

3 Divide the dyed Merino into three sections, and lay it out in three layers following the directions on page 17, steps 1 through 8.

4 Wet and felt the scarf following the directions for steps 9 through 22 on pages 18–20. Make sure that after felting the edges lay flat.

5 Stitch a white or contrasting color running down the center of the scarf (photo 1). This line will help you determine the center when cutting each

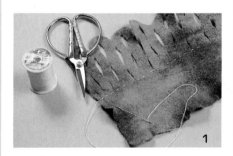

6 Cut the layout pattern on one side of the scarf up to the center thread (photo 2). After cutting about three or four rows, stretch the cuts open and

round off the outside scallops. Cut, stretch, and trim the scallops. As you continue to cut and stretch, the cut area of the scarf will start curving. Try to maintain cuts at a right angle to the middle thread. Cut all of one side, and then flip the scarf over and cut the other side.

7 Fold the scarf down the middle and arrange it in a circle as shown in photo 3 to dry. If you fold the scarf back into a circle after each wearing, you will maintain the wonderful wavy effect of the cuts.

VARIATIONS

Try cutting the scarf along the length using the same cutting pattern.

DREADNAUTS

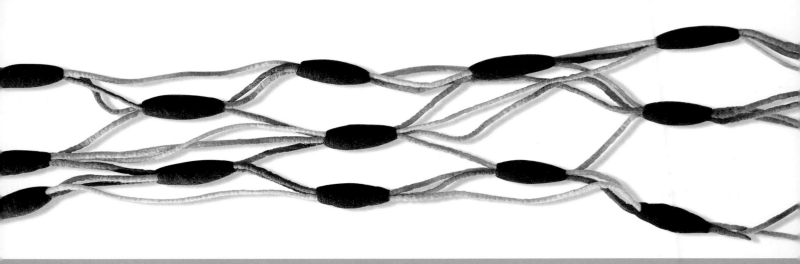

NAUTICAL NET AND DREADLOCKS, THIS UNIQUE SCARF IS CREATED WITH ROPES AND BEADS—TWO OF THE THREE-DIMENSIONAL HAND FELTED WOOL POSSIBILITIES. IT IS EASY TO WEAR AS THE BEADS CONTROL ALL THE ROPES, ALLOWING THEM TO BE MOVED AROUND FOR ADDITIONAL STYLING OPTIONS. STRIKING AS A SCARF, HEAD WRAP, OR BELT, IT IS A WEARABLE PIECE OF ART.

Supplies

4 oz (112 g) red Merino roving

16 g/1 oz yellow Merino roving

20 feet (6.1 m) of black Merino roving (for 10 ropes)

4 pencils

Ridged felt mat (see Tools on page 13)

Felting kit (page 12)

18 x 36-inch (45.7 x 91.4 cm) piece of paper or plastic

Clear cellophane tape

NOTE: *You will make all the elements of this scarf first, and then assemble them.*

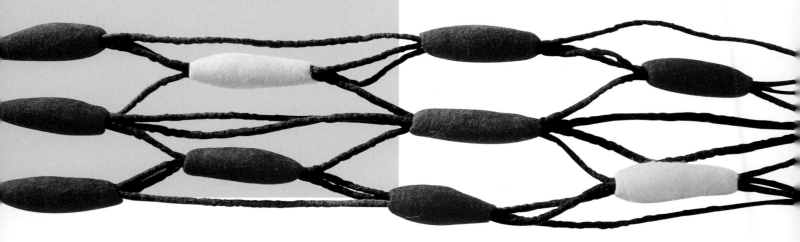

INSTRUCTIONS

1 You will begin by making 23 ball tube beads. Divide the red and yellow wool into 23 sections, each weighing .2 oz (4 g). It is easiest to make this an assembly line effort, and since each bead takes a while, plan on doing the felting over two or three evenings while watching TV. Follow the directions on page 26 for making these beads.

2 Divide the black roving and make 10 ropes following the directions on pages 27–28.

3 Draw the bead-stringing diagram (below) to scale (8 x 36 inches [20.3 x 91.4 cm]) on paper or a plastic sheet. Notice how the ropes and beads repeat their beading pattern.

4 To assemble, start threading the three beads at the end of the scarf. It helps to tightly wrap clear cellophane tape around the tips of the group of ropes of which you are threading through the beads. Once through the bead, cut off the tape, separate the ropes, and retape the next group of ropes.

5 Thread three ropes (taped together as shown in photo 1) through the top bead, the next four ropes through the middle bead, and the last three ropes through the bottom bead. Use the dull pointed end of a pencil to help push the ropes through (photo 1). Once all the ropes are through the bead, cut off all the tape.

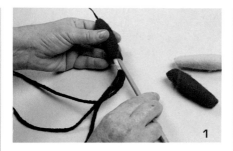

6 Lay the threaded beads and ropes on top of your beading diagram (photo 2). Follow the assembly and thread the remainder of the beads through the ropes, working from one side to the other.

7 When all the beads have been correctly threaded, make a final adjustment to the scarf by pulling the ropes to make the beads even on both sides (photo 3).

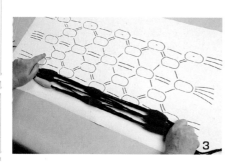

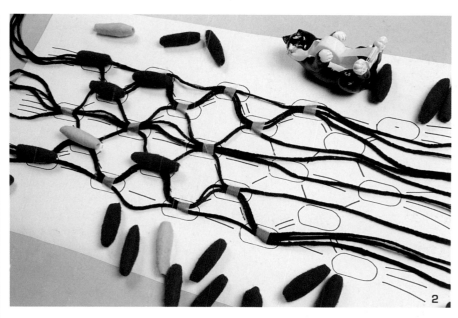

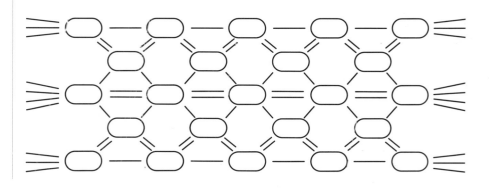

LILY PAD WRAP

THE BLENDED COLORS

IN THIS SERENE SCARF ARE REFLECTIVE OF MONET'S WATER LILY PAINTINGS, AND ARE CREATED BY DRY DYE POWDER DYEING. IT DOESN'T MATTER THE EXACT COLORS YOU ADD TO THE DYE POT, SO EXPERIMENT WITH DIFFERENT GREENS, BLUES, TURQUOISES, AND YELLOWS. THE WRAP IS SHAPED LIKE A LILY PAD, COMPLETE WITH AN ASYMMETRICAL PATTERN AND RIPPLE-STRETCHED EDGES. WITH VARIOUS BUTTONING OPTIONS, YOU WILL ENJOY THE DIF-FERENT WAYS YOU CAN BUTTON AND ARRANGE THIS PIECE AROUND YOUR SHOULDERS.

SUPPLIES

2.5 to 3 oz (70 to 84 g)* dry dye powered dyed Merino roving, 24 or 17 micron

Heavy plastic sheeting, 20 x 60 inches

Pattern (page 71) (enlarge to 70 inches long)

Felting kit (page 12)

Pliers

Steam iron

Small piece of cardboard

Pearl cotton thread, size 32, in a color to contrast with your dyed wool

Large eye needle

Buttonhole thread

*Reserve .4 oz (10 g) for the button balls

INSTRUCTIONS

1 Dye the roving according to instructions on page 34. Let dry.

2 Lay plastic sheeting over the enlarged pattern on your worktable. Trace the pattern outline with permanent marker onto the plastic.

3 Divide the dyed roving into four sections, one for each of the four layers. Lay out the first three layers according to the directions on page 17, steps 1 through 7, except start by laying the first layer from top to bottom on the pattern. Do not tuck any wool edges under yet.

4 When you come to the fourth layer, you will be laying the wool down differently. Think of each of the ends of the scarf as a circle, and lay out an " X " with wool through the circle. Then starting from the center of each circle and working outward, fill in each of the quarters formed by the X. Continue to lay the wool out to the pattern edge and to the middle of the scarf (photo 1).

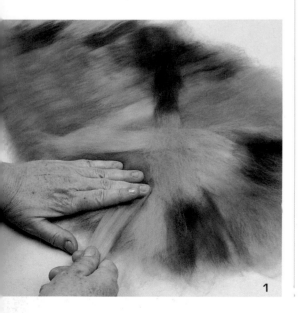

5 Tuck under the extra wool that extends beyond the pattern edge.

6 Follow the wetting and felting directions on page 18 from step 9 to the end.

7 Lay the damp scarf on the table and flatten it, pulling the edges back into the pattern shape. Then ripple stretch the edge like you are fluting a piecrust: use two fingers to hold the scarf, and two fingers to pinch and pull the ripple (see photo 2). Do this twice around, and then go over the ripples again using pliers to further pull and define the folds. You want to stretch out the felt so the ripples stay in the scarf. You may also want to iron *just the center* of the scarf with a steam iron. This helps the ripples stand out more and flattens the center. Let dry flat.

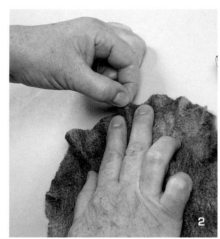

8 Divide the saved wool into five equal sections, and follow the directions on page 25 to make five small button balls (2 g each).

9 Draw and cut out a cardboard pattern for the holes, making sure that it is smaller than the button balls (photo 3).

Trace about 10 to 12 holes all over the scarf with the marker.

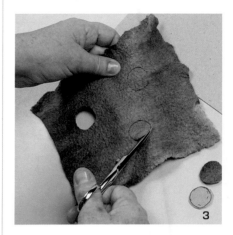

10 Cut out the holes and embroider the edges with the pearl cotton in a buttonhole stitch, as shown in photo 4. Use a single thread without any knots. Secure the thread by taking a ¾-inch (1.9 cm) "invisible" stitch through the middle of the felt fabric about ¼ inch (6 mm) around the edge of the cut hole. Pull the thread through the felt until just a short tail end is showing. Snip this off with scissors. Begin the buttonhole stitch right over the hidden thread. End the stitching the same way as you began by going back through the middle of the felt.

11 Try the scarf on to see where you want to position the button balls. Since you have made five buttons, place them in different areas so you can have a variety of ways to wear the scarf.

12 Use a doubled buttonhole thread with a big double knot at the end. Hide the knot by pushing the needle through the ball from the bottom. Push the needle back down from the top through the ball and scarf, pulling the thread tight so it makes a little indentation on the top of the ball. Make a small ½-inch (1.3 cm) stitch through the underside of the scarf, and push the needle back through the scarf to the top of the ball. Repeat, making a small stitch across the first stitch on the underside of the scarf. Finish with a double knot and pull the needle out through the side of the ball, pulling the knot into the ball (photo 5). Pull tight and snip the thread.

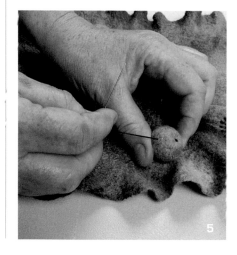

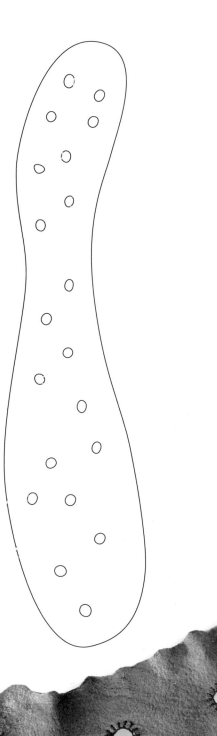

MAGIC
MUFFLER

THIS SCARF USES A BLEND OF FINE MERINO WOOL AND TUSSAH SILK. THE SILK'S REFLECTIVE PROPERTIES ADD A LUMINOUS SHINE TO THE FINISHED SCARF. DYE COLORS ARE PAINTED DIRECTLY ON THE WET FELT, AND THE FOLDED AND CLAMPED SCARF IS THEN PROCESSED IN A BLACK HOT WATER DYE BATH. WHEN THE SCARF IS RINSED, SHAPES OF BRIGHT COLORS BORDERED WITH RICH BLACK WILL AMAZE AND MYSTIFY YOU AND YOUR FRIENDS.

SUPPLIES

2.5 to 3 oz (70 to 84 g) Merino wool/tussah silk roving (a 50/50 or other percentage blend)

Felt kit (see page 12)

NOTE: *This can be a messy technique, so read through all the instructions first and have everything prepared before starting the dye painting.*

Soft Drink Mixes as Dyes

Soft drink mixes without any added sugar or sweetener can be used instead of the acid dyes. Pick different flavors for the different colors. The food colors that are used in these soft drinks make strong, bright colors on protein fibers like silk and wool, and the dyed color is fade-resistant. Just follow the same directions, including adding the acid water.

DYEING SUPPLIES

Dye kitchen and dye bath set up for black immersion dye bath (page 31)

Waterproof work area (lay down plastic and old newspapers for easy cleanup)

Citric acid or white vinegar

Dye teaspoons (¼ tsp [1.25 mL])

Glass measuring cup

Mixing spoon

60 pieces of 4-mil heavy plastic, each 3 x 3-inch (7.6 x 7.6 cm) square

Four small plastic cups

Paper towels

Thin latex type gloves

Dust mask

Four different acid dye colors or flavors of regular soft drink mix

Four 1-inch (2.5 cm) brushes

Two wooden boards, each 3 x 3 x ½ inches (7.6 x 7.6 x 1.3 cm)

Two G clamps, 14 to 16 inches (35.6 to 40.6 cm) long

Tongs

HINT: *When using white or light colored wool, a dark table covering is very useful for seeing the density of the laid out fibers. Use tailor's chalk or a white pencil to draw out your pattern lines.*

INSTRUCTIONS

1 Divide the roving into three sections, one section for each layer of the scarf. Follow the directions on page 17, steps 1 to 8 for laying out the scarf on a layout pattern of 9 x 96 inches (22.9 x 243.8 cm).

2 Wet and felt the scarf according to the basic instructions on pages 18 to 20, steps 9 through end. When finished, lay it out flat and block. The felt needs to be kept wet for the resist dyeing.

3 Prepare a black immersion acid dye bath according to directions on page 33, steps 1 through 3. Mix up the acid water by adding 1 teaspoon (5 mL) of citric acid to 2 cups (.48 L) of water. Stir well. If you're using white vinegar, add 2 tablespoons (30 mL) to 2 cups (.48 L) of water.

4 Measure and cut out the 3-inch (7.6 cm) plastic squares. Put them in a dish for easier use (photo 1).

5 Place the small plastic dye cups on paper towels as shown. Fill the cups half full of the acid water. Put on your plastic gloves and mask, and put ¼ teaspoon (1.25 mL) of dry dye powder into each cup (if you are using soft drink mixes, add the whole envelope to each cup) (photo 2). Stir well until the powder is dissolved. The plastic cup lids are handy for resting your wet paintbrush on between uses.

6 Place the dye cups, brushes, and the dish of plastic squares on your work area. Unroll the damp scarf on the plastic in front of the paint area (photo 3). Keep your gloves on!

7 Paint your dye colors however you wish, directly on the wet scarf in a 3-inch wide (7.6 cm) band down the center of the scarf (photo 4).

8 Cover one of the wooden squares with a plastic square. Pick up one end of the scarf and place the plastic-covered wooden square under the painted area near the end of the scarf (photo 5). Lay the scarf back down and place another square of plastic on the painted area of the scarf, directly over the wooden block.

9 Pick up the opposite end of the scarf and fold it in an accordion fold over the plastic square, leaving about a ½-inch (1.3 cm) border. Place another square of plastic on the painted scarf directly over the last square and fold the scarf back in the other direction (accordion-fold style) (photo 6).

Continue folding the scarf back and forth with a piece of plastic between each fold, each laid directly over the last (diagram 1). Keep moving and don't hesitate while folding, as the wet dyes will start to mix and blend.

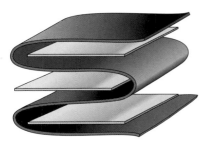

Diagram 1

10 Top off with a plastic square and the other wooden square (photo 7). Make sure the pile of painted scarf, plastic, and wooden squares are stacked directly on top of each other.

11 Attach the G clamps an equal distance from each other on the boards (photo 8). Tighten the clamps as hard as you can—the tighter the clamps, the better the resist will be. A lot of excessive dye will be dripping out of the scarf, so do this step as fast as you can. Put the clamped stack in a plastic bucket for transport to the heated dye pot.

12 Place the folded, clamped scarf in the dye pot as shown on pages 33–34, following steps 4 to 8.

13 Make sure the metal clamps have cooled before you remove the clamps, wooden boards, and plastic squares (photo 9). Rinse the scarf again in luke-warm water until the rinse water runs clear. Lay the scarf flat on the table, and block it as directed. Let dry.

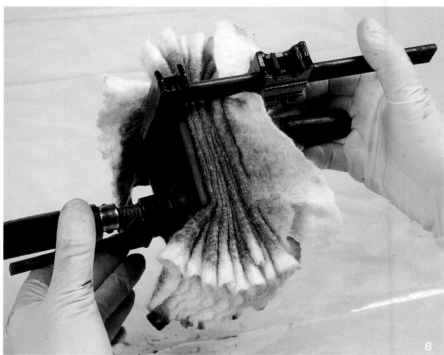

BUBBLE BOA

WOOL HAS A WONDERFUL
THERMAL SETTING PROP-
ERTY ALLOWING IT TO
HOLD A SHAPE THAT IS
SET WITH PRESSURE AND
HEAT. TAKING ADVANTAGE
OF THIS CHARACTERISTIC
CREATES A WHOLE NEW
WORLD OF SURFACE
DESIGN AND TEXTURE
TECHNIQUES. MARBLES
AND RUBBER BANDS
SHAPE THE BUBBLES ON
THIS BOUNCING SCARF,
ALTHOUGH YOU COULD
ALSO USE DRIED BEANS
OR SMALL CLEAN STONES.

SUPPLIES

2 to 2.5 oz (56 to 70 g) 24 micron
Merino wool, in your choice of color

Felting kit (page 12)

Glass marbles, dry beans, or stones
(around 150)

Small #10 size rubber bands (you can
find good ones at an orthodontist or at
farm stores where they are sold for
braiding horse manes)

TIP: *Two important keys to **Bubble
Boa** success is to let the finished scarf
dry completely before removing the
marbles, and to use the slightly thicker
24 micron Merino, which helps the
scarf retain the surface shape.*

INSTRUCTIONS

1 Following the directions on page 17
for steps 1 through 8, draw a layout
pattern of 9 x 96 inches (22.9 x 243.8
cm). Divide your wool into three sections, and lay it out in three layers.

2 Felt the scarf according to the
basic felting directions on pages 18–20
(steps 9 through 22). Keep the scarf
damp for wrapping the marbles. If you
wish to rubber band the marbles on
another day, then let the scarf dry flat

now and just before you are ready to
continue, soak the dry scarf in warm
water for 20 minutes.

3 Gather your marbles, rubber bands,
and damp scarf. Place a marble under
the scarf and tightly wrap a rubber
band three times around it (photo 1).
Rubber band the marbles for the entire
scarf all at the same time. Remember,
the scarf needs to stay damp throughout this process, so place it in a plastic
bag if you need more time.

1

4 Prepare a clear, hot water bath following directions on page 34. When the correct temperature has been reached, put the scarf in the bath and set the timer (photo 2). It is okay if the water bath boils. Stir it every 10 minutes.

5 After the water bath, remove the scarf and let it dry either on a towel or a waterproof surface, setting a fan to move air around it. Dry the scarf fast, especially if you used beans, as they can start to rot if left more than a day.

6 Once the scarf is dry, remove the rubber bands and marbles (photo 3). You can snip the rubber bands, but be very careful not to cut through the scarf. Stretch and shake the scarf out a bit, and it is ready to wear.

Variations

Variations on this scarf are almost overwhelming. The instructions call for the use of a clear (no dye) hot water bath, but you could just as well over-dye the scarf in an immersion dye bath (see page 33), creating circles where the rubber bands were and spots where the marbles were. My friend Joke in Holland, a fine felter, loves working with this technique and has created many different arrangements of the "marbled" bubbles on the surface of a scarf. Try just one line of bubbles up a side, or all the bubbles grouped at one end, or fold the bubbles in half, creating a scalloped edge. The wrapped marbles can also be resist-capped with a layer of plastic, and then dyed to retain the original color of the wool.

NOTE: *For a different look, try carefully taking out the marbles before the scarf is totally dry and then stretching the bubbles out more.*

Leiko Uchiyama-Vergain

UNTITLED, 2006
60⅞ x 9¼ inches (155 x 23.5 cm)
Wool, dye; wet felted
PHOTO BY ARTIST
PRIVATE COLLECTION

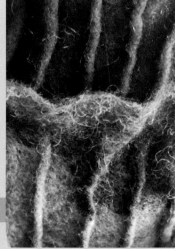

Simone Edwards

FUR FELTED SCARF, 2006
140 x 25 inches (355.6 x 63.5 cm)
Merino wool, silk, mohair, flax fibers;
felting needle technique, brushed
PHOTO BY ARTIST

Ewa Kuniczak

ORCHID CASCADE NECKPIECE OR BELT, 2006
45 x 8 inches (114.3 x 20.3 cm)
Felted merino wool, felted millinery wire; hand-dyed, wet felted, flowers stiffened with textile medium
PHOTO BY ARTIST

Natalya Pinchuk

MULTIPLYING LIKE KUDZU, 2006
96 inches (243.8 cm)
Wool, found sweaters
PHOTO BY ARTIST

Karen Miknas

UNTITLED, 2007
62⅞ x 5⅞ inches (160 x 15 cm)
Felted silk and Merino wool, tussah
silk, boucle wool; dyed
PHOTO BY GILL ORSMAN

Lori Flood

WAVY PETAL SCARF, 2006
84 x 15 inches (213.4 x 38.1 cm)
Merino wool; wet felted
PHOTO BY TOM MCCOLLEY

Catherine O'Leary

DREAMER, 2006
62⅞ x 23³⁄₁₆ inches (160 x 60 cm)
Merino wool, silk cotton; hand felted
PHOTO BY SHANE HOGARTH

Joke van Zinderen

UNTITLED, 2006
78⅝ x 13¾ inches (200 x 35 cm)
Cobweb, extra fine merino; shibori dyed
PHOTO BY ARTIST

Lisa Klakulak

BOUND BUTTONS SHAWL, 2006
65 x 16 inches (165.1 x 40.6 cm)
Merino and Finn/Rambolet fleece, silk fabric, wood buttons; naturally dyed with cochineal insects and walnut hulls, wet felted by hand
PHOTO BY JOHN LUCAS

Ulrieke Benner

COLOR LADDER AND WINDSPRITE, 2005–2006
Longest: 15 x 2¾ inches (38.1 x 7 cm)
Wool, silk, thread; wet felted
PHOTO BY JOHN CAMERON

84

Jackie Mirabel

CRUELLA, 2007
115 x 51 inches (292.1 x 129.5 cm)
Nuno (Merino wool, silk), embellishments;
hand dyed, stitched
PHOTO BY STEVE FENTON

Joke van Zinderen

UNTITLED, 2006
78⅝ x 19⅝ inches (200 x 50 cm)
Cobweb, extra fine Merino; shibori dyed
PHOTO BY ARTIST
PRIVATE COLLECTION

Lisa Klakulak

BREAST FENCE, 2004
36 x 20 inches (91.4 x 50.8 cm)
Merino and Finn/Rambolet fleece, mohair yarn, mettler sewing
thread, waxed linen; wet felted by hand, naturally dyed with
osage heartwood and indigo, hand and machine stitched
PHOTO BY JOHN LUCAS
PRIVATE COLLECTION

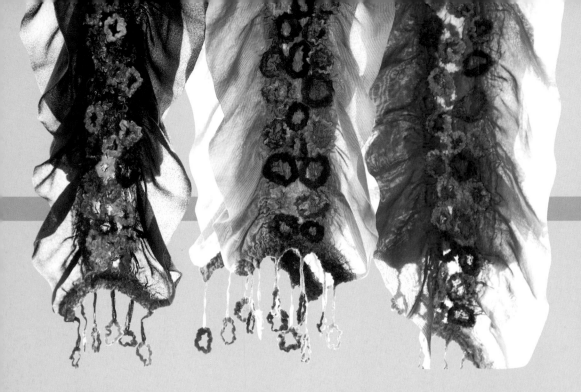

Lynn Ocone

PARTY SCARVES, 2006
73 x 7½ inches (185.4 x 19.1 cm)
Wool and silk roving with woven silk; wet felted
PHOTO BY MICHAEL MACCASKEY

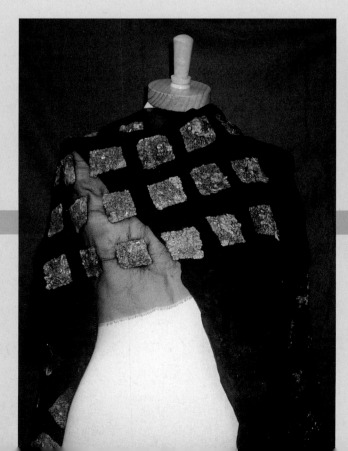

Elizabeth Armstrong

ILLUMINATION, 2006
55 x 39⁵⁄₁₆ inches (140 x 100 cm)
Merino, soy silk, silk chiffon; hand dyed, wet felted
PHOTO BY ARTIST

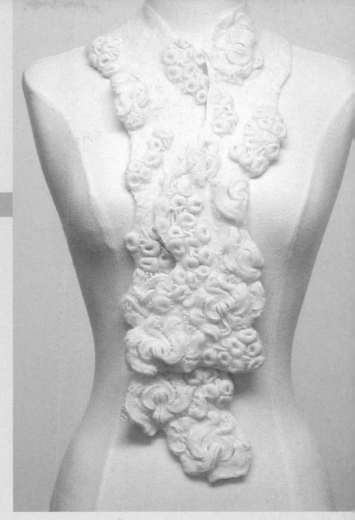

Liz Clay

SCULPTURED SCARF, 2007
43¼ x 4¾ inches (110 x 12 cm)
Silk, merino, cashmere with
embroidered wool lace;
hand felted
PHOTO BY ARTIST

Lene Nielsen

EVENING STAR, 1997
149⁵⁄₁₆ × 37⁵⁄₁₆ inches (380 x 95 cm)
Tussah silk/merino blend; felted using a
variety of rolling techinques
PHOTO BY KIRSTEN NIJKAMP

Ulrieke Benner

WORDS, SASHAY AND LINE SPIRAL WITH ANTLER FRINGE, 2004–2006
Longest: 12 x 3¹¹⁄₁₆ inches (30.5 x 9.3 cm)
Wool, silk, dye; wet felted
PHOTO BY JOHN CAMERON

Alexander Pilin

THE WARM GRASS, 2000
78⅝ x 51¹⁄₁₆ inches (200 x 130 cm)
Felt lace, natural color wool
PHOTO BY E. AKSIONOV

Breanna Rockstad-Kincaid

SPIKEY BOA, 2005
60 x 1 inches
(152.4 x 2.5 cm)
Australian Merino wool;
wet felted, rolling
technique
PHOTO BY JOHN LUCAS

Breanna Rockstad-Kincaid

BOBBLE NECKPIECE #1, 2005
54 x 1 inches (137.2 x 2.5 cm)
Merino and mohair wool; wet felted, seamless
construction
PHOTO BY JOHN LUCAS

Breanna Rockstad-Kincaid

VINE BOA, 2005
64 x 3 x 3 inches (162.6 x 7.6 x 7.6 cm)
Australian Merino wool; wet felted, rolling
technique, fruit felted, stitched
PHOTO BY JOHN LUCAS

Catherine O'Leary

UNTITLED, 2006
$31^{7}/_{16}$ x $15^{3}/_{4}$ inches (80 x 40 cm)
Merino wool, silk; hand felted
PHOTO BY SHANE HOGARTH

Catherine O'Leary

UNTITLED, 2006
$58^{15}/_{16}$ x $19^{11}/_{16}$ inches (150 x 50 cm)
Merino wool, silk; hand felted
PHOTO BY SHANE HOGARTH

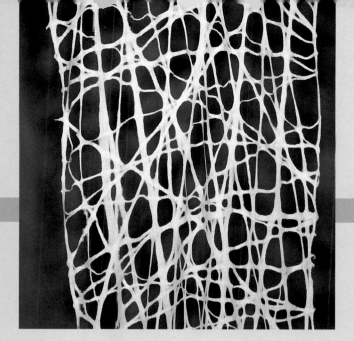

Lene Nielsen

MORNING MIST, 1998
125¾ x 35⅜ inches (320 x 90 cm)
Shappesilk, merino blend; felted using a variety
of rolling techinques
PHOTO BY KIRSTEN NIJKAMP

Liz Clay

MULTI-LAYER BOA, 2006
72¹¹⁄₁₆ x 11¹³⁄₁₆ inches (185 x 30 cm)
Merino wool, cashmere, silk; hand felted
PHOTO BY ARTIST

Christine White

MINT MOCHA ACCORDION SCARF, 2006
79¾ x 12 inches (203 x 30.5 cm)
Finn sheep wool, silk; wet felted, heat-set pleats
PHOTO BY JOHN POLAK PHOTOGRAPHY

JORIE JOHNSON

now, daily, I put into practice optical color blending concepts while layering wool and overlapping auxiliary materials to prepare my fabrics.

After Wheaton I was accepted into the Textile Design department at the Rhode Island School of Design, where another Finnish professor, Maria Tulokas, taught me the basics of silkscreen printing on fabric. As fate would have it, there in 1977 I saw a notice posted on the textile department door introducing a study program for Americans in Scandinavia. Maybe it was a yearning to follow my own Scandinavian roots, or perhaps it was due to the great respect I had for my professors that I decided to study abroad for a year—which ultimately turned out to be a life abroad.

Raised in the home of a wool and fiber merchant west of Boston, Massachusetts, I was exposed to fine quality woolen fabrics and textiles at a very young age. I attended Wheaton College in Massachusetts, where I studied two-dimensional color theory under Väinö Kola, who had been a student at Yale University under the tutelage of renowned German colorist, Professor Josef Albers. My studies with Väinö proved priceless because even

My first December in Kuopio, Finland, I attended a three-day felt boot-making course in the department of "Special Techniques," geared toward students learning to become teachers. Logically, crafting a pair of boots means making two pieces that look alike and have the same fit…quite an ambitious first project to tackle in an unknown technique that was being dished out in an

unfamiliar language. Looking back (with a good laugh) I credit that long boot-making session in Kuopio as being the point from which I got so involved in feltmaking.

The survival technique of indigenous peoples living in demanding or severe environments has always interested me. This includes how they live, what they eat, and what they wear to protect themselves from the elements. After spending some time experiencing the harsh living conditions of nomadic families in Outer Mongolian, I found that I no longer held a romantic view of feltmaking—especially after my Western upbringing. What I did find heartwarming, though, was the deep appreciation we shared for wool, which the heavens have passed onto us through its messenger, the sheep.

Living in Japan since 1989 I have crossed the boundary of wool being used solely for warmth, and have plunged into free-form creation with my university students, and creating felted designs to adorn my 21st century contemporary clients. Through this publication and others that I have contributed to, I have come to realize that I am an ambassador of wool, boasting its admirable, enthralling, and truly lovable felting qualities.

Josie Johnson

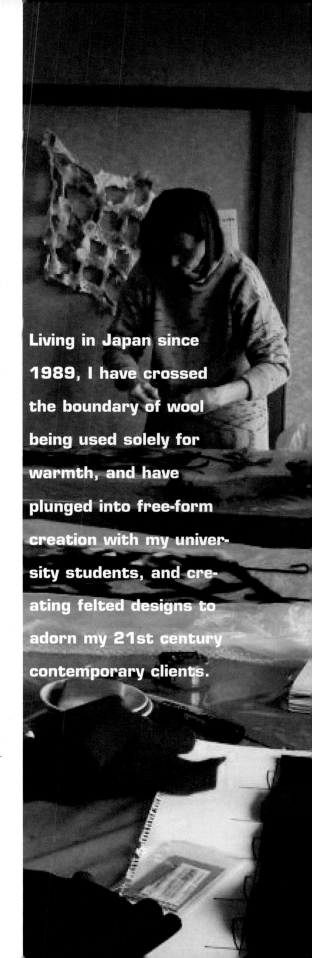

Living in Japan since 1989, I have crossed the boundary of wool being used solely for warmth, and have plunged into free-form creation with my university students, and creating felted designs to adorn my 21st century contemporary clients.

DIP DYED
PARTY

SCARF

HOW FINE WOOL FIBER READILY
PIERCES SHEER FABRICS DURING
THE ENTANGLING PROCESS AND
ACTUALLY JOINS TWO PIECES OF
FABRIC TOGETHER WITH NON-
FELTING "PARTY STREAMERS"
CAUGHT IN BETWEEN.

NOTE: *Silk "stains" easily, so to avoid graying the fabric, DO NOT use hot felting solution. As dyed silk also weakens and runs in alkaline solutions. use a milder concentration felting solution.*

TIP: *To see whether the metallic and polyester threads you chose will be visible through the silk fabric after felting, make a small sample following the instructions as if you were making the larger project.*

Supplies

White, lightweight, sheer silk fabric with drape*,
35½ x 60 inches (84 x 150 cm)

6 g white 64 Merino (or finer wool) roving

10 g black 64 Merino (or finer wool) roving

8 g bright pastels 64 Merino (in total)

Black acid dye

Novelty threads, in small amounts, 100% polyester, rayon, and metallic or Lurex (Do not use any yarns with wool or mohair as you do not want these threads to felt into the silk fabric)

Jorie's Additional Tools (page 13)

Polyester mesh

Felting kit (page 12)

1½-inch (3.8 cm) diameter polystyrene rolling rod

*Such as silk georgette or chiffon

95

INSTRUCTIONS

1 Following the manufacturer's safety instructions on the package, dip dye ⅔ to ¾ of the silk fabric's length to produce a gradation (see acid dyeing instructions for silk fabric on page 35). A black acid dye was thinned to produce the dark gray of this scarf. After dyeing, rinse the silk well, spin out the excess moisture, and leave to dry.

2 Steam iron the fabric to square it off. Fold it down the center making it half as wide, and steam set a center crease down the length. Center the folded scarf on a sheet of bubble wrap that is about 3 inches (7.6 cm) wider on both sides of the folded fabric. Open the scarf up away from you. Keep the fabric dry throughout the design preparation stages.

3 Lay one ¾-inch (1.9 cm) row of black Merino down the entire length of the fabric, about a ¼-inch (6 mm) away from the center crease. Leave 1 inch (2.5 cm) free from the edge at the white end. Lay down just enough black Merino until you cannot see the fabric underneath.

4 Finish the row by laying down enough white Merino to fill the final inch (2.5 cm) and to extend beyond the silk fabric edge another 2½ inches (6.4 cm). Fill in this section across the entire edge, then lay a second horizontal layer perpendicular to the first. Follow this by a third lengthwise layer. Fill in the 2½ inch (6.4 cm) edge with short white Merino tufts (photo 1). If the fibers are too long to fit, cut the tufts in half. Repeat the same process for the opposite end, using black Merino.

5 On the opposite selvedge edge, lay down a narrow ¾-inch (1.9 cm) row of black Merino just inside the selvedge. Leave 1 inch (2.5 cm) of fabric along the edge free for the entire length of this side.

6 About every 6½ inches (16.5 cm), use dark yet brightly colored Merino to make a ¾-inch (1.9 cm) wide cross row. The rows don't have to be a solid color; you can join two or three colors. Lay down just enough wool so that the silk fabric can no longer be seen. Extend each row up to the black Merino, and cut it off to make a square joint. Continue on the other side of the black Merino to the edge of the fabric, allowing about an inch of brightly colored wool to cross over the fabric's edge (photo 2) to make a tag.

7 Evenly distribute five groupings of metallic yarn (each group consisting of two or three gold metallic threads laid together) lengthwise. In between each metallic grouping, lay a fancy synthetic novelty yarn (photo 3).

8 To secure the threads in place, repeat the crosswise color layering, laying down just enough wool until the shine of the metallic thread is lost. Also, lay two more fine layers of white and black at their respective scarf ends, until the shine of the threads disappears (photo 4).

9 Lift up the remaining half of the fabric and carefully cover the design (photo 5). Georgette is a stretchy fabric, so take care to align the edges properly and then check to see if any wool has shifted position. Carefully cover everything with a polyester mesh, and wet the lines of wool with cool to lukewarm felting solution.

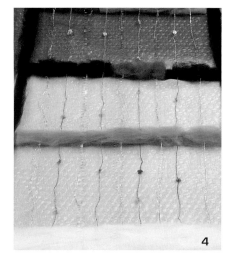

Massage the felting solution throughout the scarf to evenly wet the wool.

10 Remove the mesh and cover with painter's plastic. Carefully roll up onto a 1½-inch-diameter (3.8 cm) polystyrene rolling rod, then in a cotton sheet, tying off both ends. Roll for 100 counts, exerting very light pressure in the beginning rounds.

11 Open up the bundle and check that the wool has not shifted out of place and that there are no wrinkles. Roll up from the opposite end and tie off. Roll for another 100 counts. Open up the bundle and check again that the fabric is smooth, then continue by rolling 200 counts per direction. Flip the bubble wrap, scarf, and plastic sheet over, and roll 200 counts from both ends again (for a total of 500 counts from both directions).

12 Remove the plastic and rub the surface with plastic bag-covered hands. Rub in the direction in which the fibers were laid down. Remove the bubble sheet and replace it with painter's plastic. Fold the scarf in

thirds on top of itself, with plastic between the layers, and then roll it up widthwise on a ¾-inch (1.9 cm) diameter pipe. Roll for 200 counts, and then open the fabric to eliminate any creasing. Refold it in different areas, and then roll again from the opposite edge for another 200 counts.

13 Throw onto the tabletop 40 times. Lay the scarf on the sheet and gather two of the widthwise colored wool stripes (photo 6). Roll inside the sheet for 40 counts with pressure just on the wool areas. Continue the next two stripes in the same way until all have been rolled. Do not roll the bottom black or white edges.

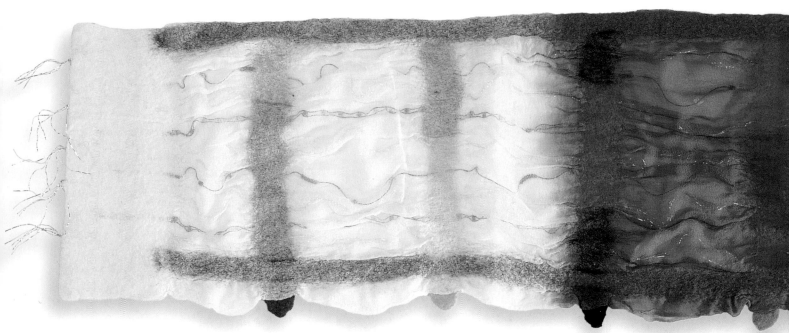

A variation is shown in color combinations.

14 Stretch out the little tags of color at the selvedge, as well as the opposite folded-over edge to prevent it from doubling over and sticking to itself (photo 7). Keep working the width until it measures about 9 x 50 inches (22.9 x 127 cm) in length.

7

15 Rinse well in warm water, then soak in a mild vinegar solution for five minutes. Spin or wring out excess moisture, and hang to dry. Trim the metallic threads at both ends of the scarf to roughly 2 inches (5 cm). Carefully steam iron the felt area, while avoiding any Lurex or polyester threads that might melt or change color with heat. Have a great evening out!

FALLEN LEAVES COLLAR

WHEN I AM OUT WALKING ON A

BRISK AUTUMN DAY AND SEE

LOVELY FALLEN LEAVES JUST OFF

THEIR BRANCHES, THEY MAKE

ME WISH I COULD DRESS UP IN

THEIR BEAUTIFUL COLORS AND

SHAPES. THIS AUTUMN COLLAR

WAS DESIGNED TO INCORPORATE

COLOR STUDY, BASIC TWO-

DIMENSIONAL FORM MAKING, AND

NEEDLE FELTING POSSIBILITIES.

SUPPLIES

50 g 58 crossbred or 64 Merino Color A*, roving

50 g 58 crossbred or 64 Merino Color B*, roving

Mohair novelty yarn (for leaf vein motif), small amounts

Hand carders (or a pair of wire dog brushes)

3¾ x 4¼-inch (9.5 x 10.8cm) oval plastic food container (or suitable substitute)

Cord making supplies (see page 29)

Felting kit (page 12)

Block of dense rubber foam

#36 felting needle

Jorie's Additional Tools (see page 13)

Rolling pipe

Needle-nose pliers

*Choose the same quality wool for both colors. You will only use 35 g of each color for the leaves, leaving plenty to make a cord. You will likely have some wool left over.

NOTE: *To produce rich, well-blended colors for the leaves, hand carders are used to facilitate the mixing process. Before deciding which two colors to work with, make some quick tests like those detailed in Hand Carding Practice and Color Sampling (page 36).*

INSTRUCTIONS

1 Measure and separate a 45-inch (114.3 cm) length strand from each of the two selected colors. Make one cord in color A and one cord in color B using the instructions given on page 29.

2 For ease in calculating the proportional weight of the wool to be blended you will be working in portions totaling 10g. Weigh out portions of each color in the following amounts: 1 g, 3 g, 5 g, 7 g, 9 g, and 10 g. Start color blending by pairing 1 g color A/9 g color B; 3 g color A/7 g color B, 5 g color A/5 g color B, 7 g color A/3 g color B, and 9 g color A/1 g color B (photo 1).

3 Following the directions on page 37, color blend each pair of colors together, creating five blended colors. Make sure that the color progression along the seven leaves is consistent. Once you are satisfied with your blended color gradation, set the piles of wool aside.

4 Card the solid color A wool (10 g) into the same fluffy condition as the blended colors. Do the same with the solid color B wool.

5 Use a 3¾ x 4¼-inch (9.5 x 10.8 cm) oval plastic food container (or suitable substitute) to help create a prefelted oval leaf shape. Divide the carded pile of solid color A wool into six or more smaller clouds. Make the first layer by pulling off short lengths of fibers and placing them into your form across the shorter width, just to the walls of the form. Lay the fibers from the second pile perpendicularly across the first layer, striving for an

even thickness. Add the third layer widthwise.

6 Spread open the dry ends of the color A cord as shown in photo 2. Lay both cord ends 2 inches (5 cm) apart on top of the three layers of wool.

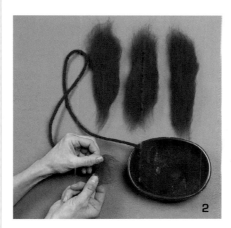

7 Place the remaining three layers into the form in alternating directions (photo 3). Cut the fibers in half if they are too long.

8 Feel with your fingertips that the dry wool is evenly dispersed. Sprinkle enough hot felting solution into the form to completely wet the fibers. After running your fingertips over a bar of soap, gently rub the wool back and forth for two minutes. Do not allow the wool to run up the edge of the container—push it back down the side of the form.

9 Flip the wool over in the plastic form, being careful not to dislodge the cord ends, and continue rubbing for two more minutes. If there is too much liquid or a lot of suds, remove excess moisture with a towel. Flip the oval over again and continue massaging for a total of five minutes. Remove the wool from the form. Apply a bit of hot felting solution or soap, and work the edge of the leaf by massaging the perimeter with your fingertips. Elongate the leaf about 1 inch (2.5 cm) by pressing with the weight of the your palm of one hand and pulling with the opposite hand.

10 Make the solid color B leaf with its cord by repeating steps 5 through 9 above. Prepare the five remaining blended color leaves in the same manner. Spin out any excess moisture or roll the leaves in a clean towel and leave them to dry completely.

11 Place a leaf onto a thick block of dense foam rubber. While holding the felting needle in the vertical position, gently stab at the mohair yarn for about 10 stabs per ½ inch (1.3 cm) of yarn (photo 4). Hold the yarn with light tension.

12 Repeat this for all the leaves, except for the solid color A and solid color B ones. For those two, run the yarn off the edge of the leaf, tightly twist it back on itself, and needle felt it back into the spine 1 inch (2.5 cm) up from the edge, forming a stem, and cut. Needle felt a vein motif into the backside of the leaf as well. Continue needle felting veins off the main spine (photo 5).

13 To join the leaves together, first use a toothbrush to rough up some loose fibers on the underside of the tip and the front side of the stem areas, about 1 inch (2.5 cm) from the edges. Overlap the leaves 1¼ inches (3.2 cm), placing the tip over the stem area of the next consecutive colored leaf. Needle felt the overlapping area (photo 6). Flip the leaves over as you join them, and needle the same area of the underside.

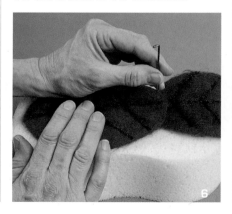

14 Lay the string of leaves on a piece of bubble wrap. Cover with netting and thoroughly wet with hot felting solution and soap. Cover with a piece of thin plastic, and roll up around a pipe, then in a piece of cloth or towel. Secure both ends.

15 Roll for 50 counts. Open up the bundle, check the design, and rub the surface of each leaf with a bit of soap and your hands covered in plastic bags. Roll again for 50 counts from the opposite direction. Open up the bundle and stretch out the leaves lengthwise, being careful not to detach any. Apply hot felting solution when necessary.

16 Roll the collar widthwise six to eight times in opposite directions, flipping it over in between rolls. Roll lengthwise in various directions until you are satisfied with the size, feel, and quality of the felt. Excluding the ties, your collar should now measure about 3½ x 32 inches (8.9 x 81 cm).

17 Use a sharp pair of scissors to snip ½ inch (1.3 cm) into the edge of the solid color B leaf, between the veins in five places (photo 7) Rub some soap on your index finger, and work the slit areas (photo 8) until

they felt open and form a jagged leaf shape. Choose six places on the next leaf to cut, and work these areas as you did the last leaf. In this collar we have left three leaves uncut.

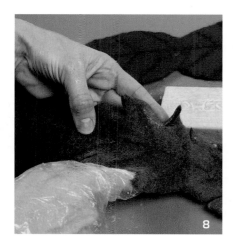

Continue cutting and shaping with your finger until you are satisfied with your combination of leaf shapes. Use a pair of needle-nose pliers to help stretch out and shape each leaf.

18 Roll the collar up on itself without a rod, and close it tightly by wrapping a cotton sheet around it. Roll the bundle for 30 counts; open and reverse from the other end for another 30 counts. Stretch out the leaves.

19 Rinse well, washing out all the soap, and leave to soak in a conditioned bath for five to 10 minutes. Rinse, spin, or wring out excess moisture in a clean towel. Steam iron flat, and leave to dry.

Design Options

This collar is of substantial weight, allowing it to also be worn as a belt—certain to complement any sweater dress.

For a longer or wider scarf with twice as many smaller and thinner leaves, divide each blended 10 g portion in half and make twice as many leaves. You can even mix wool to highlight parts of leaves with other blended colors, like mustard yellow or yellow green, making your design more realistic with practice.

Other shape variations can be made with large cookie cutters or small cake pans as long as you remember to adapt the required wool amounts to match the size of the form. Keep your eyes open for interesting forms that come your way.

FATHER'S DAY
BRAIDED MUFFLER

THIS SCARF HAS A SUBSTRUCTURE OF A FLAT BRAID. YOU MIGHT FIND THIS TRADITIONAL BRAID IN SOUTH AMERICA, MADE FROM COTTON AND USED AS A DONKEY HALTER, IN NORWAY MADE FROM TIGHTLY SPUN WOOL YARN FOR BOOT TIES; OR IN JAPAN CREATED FROM VERY FINE SILK THREADS FOR AN OBI SASH CORD. HERE, THINLY SEPARATED WOOL ROVING IS SUBSTITUTED TO PRODUCE A NICE GIFT FOR DAD.

SUPPLIES

90-inch (228.6 cm) length (approximately 36 g) of color A (fine gray silk Merino wool with a small amount of black wool and white silk fibers blended in), 7 strands divided from roving

60-inch (152.4 cm) length (approximately 44 g) of color B (hemlock greens 58 crossbred), 6 strands divided from roving

30-inch (76.2 cm) length (approximately 15 g) of color C (brick reds 58 crossbred), 6 strands divided from roving

Jorie's Additional Tools (see page 13)

Polyester mesh

Steam iron

Sander and safety equipment (see Selecting a Sander and Sander Safety on page 14)

Felting kit (page 12)

Narrow rolling rod

NOTE: *For ease of use this project requires wool carded and prepared in the form of roving (narrow "pencil" roving may be substituted). The length of the strand is more important than the weight, as sometimes just weighing out the wool may not give you the necessary length. With this technique, once the color sequence is decided and the braiding process initiated, you can add on wool strands forever—never stopping, continuing to braid for miles.*

INSTRUCTIONS

1 Select your colors and prepare the strands according to the instructions for the Practice Sample Braid on page 38. Alternating colors A and B, lay down six pairs, then one more strand of A. Align the ends of the gray and green strands at one end. Place a wide weight over the area toward the far end of the green strands in the area where the gray strands run on 30 inches (76.2 cm) longer. After the front half is braided you will flip the work around and create a gradated effect by adding the 30-inch (76.2 cm) red strands onto the green strands.

2 Proceed with braiding following the Sample Braid instructions. To facilitate the braiding process, once one woven cycle is complete, shift the braid to a smooth corner of your worktable so that the strands hang off the table's edge, with six strands on one side and seven on the other.

3 Braid until the lengths of the green and gray strands run out. Flip the scarf around carefully and turn it over. Tighten the area of the strands that was originally under the weight, and continue now toward the end of the green strands.

4 When the length of a green strand starts to run out, add to it with a red one. The easiest time to do this is when a green strand is due to become a weft strand (photo 1), or you can slide in a strand at any point by gently lifting a cross weft or two with your finger. Keep the thickness of the joint consistent with the rest of the strand.

5 Work to the end of the strands, and square off the corners by braiding over or under one less strand each time until the last edge strand crosses only one warp strand (photo 2). Repeat for the opposite end. The muffler should measure about 8 x 68 inches (20.3 x 172.7 cm), excluding the fringe.

6 Stabilize both ends of the muffler before felting. To do this, use thick thread and stitch two lines of basting stitches straight across the muffler, as seen in photo 67 on page 41).

7 To make the fringe, separate the individual strands and pull off any length that is too long, and add on extra wool to those that feel too thin. To keep them separate during the felting and rolling process, slip a piece of painter's plastic between them (photo 3) and pin it in place until the felting starts.

8 Check the surface of the muffler closely on both sides, and spread out the strands to close any openings in the areas where the strands pass over each other.

9 Position the braided muffler in the center of a piece of bubble wrap, leaving about 4 inches (10.2 cm) free at both ends, and a bit less at the sides. Pull on the edges to perfect the shape of the muffler.

10 Spray the surface of the muffler with hot water in an area about 12 inches (30.5 cm) wide and equal to a couple of lengths of your sanding machine pad. Cover the sprayed area with a piece of polyester mesh to stabilize the fibers. Being careful not to melt the bubble wrap, apply a hot steam iron to the mesh and wool to further moisten and heat the wool (photo 4).

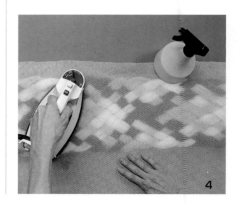

These three scarves show how easy it is to produce endless design results simply by making substitutions in color sequencing, materials, or fringe ends.

11 You will now be placing and working the sander in different directions. Start by holding the sander in the horizontal direction, and sand all the area heated in step 10 for three seconds. Lift the mesh off the wool to avoid further possible joining of the wool into the mesh. Replace the mesh and rotate the sander 90°. Cover the area with the sander again, but this time extend the sanding time to five seconds. Finally, repeat the process, turning the sander on the diagonal. Repeat for the opposite diagonal direction. Consider this one full set (four directional passes) over a 12-inch (30.5 cm) area.

12 Remove the mesh. See how well and quickly the sander initiates the entangling and stabilization of the wool (photo 5) Repeat steps 10 and 11 for the entire scarf length. Turn the muffler over and repeat for the reverse side.

5

13 Once you're finished sanding, remove the stabilizing threads at either end. Thoroughly moisten the muffler with hot felting solution, and use your hands to massage both sides in the diagonal direction for 20 counts per two-hand width section.

14 Wind the muffler lengthwise around a narrow rolling rod and inside a sheet of plastic. Roll in 200-count sessions from various directions, until the final length has shrunk to approximately 60 inches (127 cm). Fold into thirds and roll widthwise inside plastic a couple of times.

15 With plastic bags over your hands, and warm felting solution and soap, work the edges of the muffler between the fingers and palm of your closed hand. To perfect the shape and edges, continue hand agitation diagonally and "pulling" in any areas that might be wider than others. Continue the various shrinking methods above until the muffler measures about 6½ x 59 inches (16.5 x 149.8 cm).

16 Knead the muffler while rinsing it in hot water, then gently wring out the excess liquid. Leave the muffler in a conditioned bath for five to 10 minutes; rinse, spin, or roll out extra moisture. Use a steam iron to press and reshape the muffler. Leave flat to dry.

HONEYCOMB SCARF

I DEVELOPED THIS PROJECT IN

2003 DURING A ONE-MONTH HOSPITAL STAY WHEN I REALIZED THAT THE MIND MUST KEEP MOVING EVEN IF THE HIPS NEED TO STAY PUT FOR A WHILE. USING VARIOUS ODDS AND ENDS OF LEFTOVER HOSPITAL EQUIPMENT, AND WITH THE LOYAL AID OF ONE ASSISTANT, I MANAGED TO TURN A PRIVATE ROOM INTO MY STUDIO AWAY FROM HOME, AND SO CREATED THIS SCARF. DUE TO ITS UNIQUE CONSTRUCTION, THE INSIDE COLORS CAN BE SEEN— A STUNNING EFFECT THAT PROMPTS MANY ADMIRERS TO ASK, "IS THAT KNITTED OR CROCHETED?"

SUPPLIES

45 to 55 g of fine Merino, crossbred, Falkland, OR Pencil roving (all the same quality, and in several colors)

1⅛-inch (2.9 cm) diameter "giant" bubble wrap, 16 x 80-inch (40.6 cm x 203.2 cm) piece*

Felting kit (page 12)

Jorie's Additional Tools (see page 13)

Narrow plastic rod

*If you can't find a long enough piece of bubble wrap, machine stitch pieces together. Be sure to keep a consistent distance between the bubbles.

SCARF MEASUREMENTS

Outline starting size: 9¼ x 65½ inches (23.5 x 166.5 cm)
Finished size: 5 x 50 inches (12.7 x 127 cm)

NOTE: *Try making a small "hot pad" first using several different wool qualities and colors.*

INSTRUCTIONS

1 Check for consistent fineness, and subdivide the wool into eight or 12 strands. Prepare several colors at the same time. Start by dividing a length of roving in half and half again, as was done for the Practice Sample Braid on page 38.

2 On the smooth side of the bubble wrap, mark the outline of the scarf in large black circles (photo 1). Be careful; it's imperative that you avoid popping any bubbles within the scarf area.

3 As you work, thoroughly wet and keep wetting the troughs around the bumps with felting solution, as the wool will quickly absorb the liquid. Carefully push (not twist) the wool strands around the bumps in an orderly manner (photo 2). Work only in one row direction at a time. In photo 3, you can see that the turquoise wool has already been laid down in every other row, and that the black is running in horizontal stripes in a zigzag pattern down the row and back again, forming figure eights.

4 After laying one-third of the scarf length with white on every other row, fill in the remaining in-between rows with red strands. Then continue with the turquoise and black colors, wetting with hot felting solution as needed.

5 Next lay the entire lengthwise-running layer in a gradation of blues and purples on top of the readied widthwise stripes (photo 4). You may find this more difficult to do well as the space between the bumps differs in the lengthwise direction.

6 Be sure that the continuous fibers crossing each other create a strong matrix. Depending on the thickness of the strands, you may find it necessary to lay more than the one layer of wool in either direction. If the wool is too thick or there is too much of it piled up, the strands will start to slip off the bumps. Keep pushing the wool carefully around the bumps while applying lots of hot felting solution.

7 Thoroughly wet the entire surface of the wool with hot felting solution, and push all the wool into the troughs around the bumps. Place a piece of painter's plastic on top, and roll up the bubble wrap around a narrow plastic pipe. Wind in a sheet and tie off well, but not too tightly.

8 Roll 200 counts. Open, rewind from the opposite end, and roll for another 200 counts. Keep rolling with the bubble side up until you notice that the wool is shrinking and starting to slip off the bumps. Rub the surface well with your hands and hot felting solution. Carefully slip off the scarf.

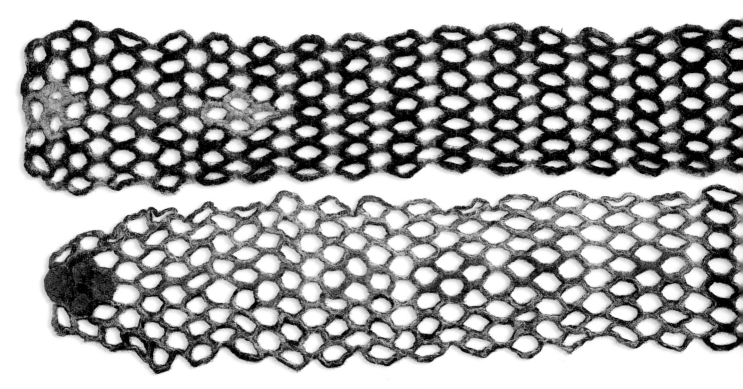

9 Roll the scarf around a hard rod and inside plastic until the fabric is strong enough to throw onto the tabletop. Throw 20 times.

10 When shrunk to the desired size, rinse out the felting solution in hot water while kneading the scarf. Spin or wring out any excess moisture, and leave the scarf in a conditioned bath for 5 to 10 minutes. Rinse again, spin, and iron into shape. Lay flat to dry.

Design Options

For this scarf, I kept to a systematic design in order to introduce the technique, but you can easily isolate areas and make a variety of ring, clover, and diamond designs.

GRANNY WARNER'S
LACE SHAWL

AS A CHILD THERE WASN'T

ANYTHING MORE FASCINAT-
ING ABOUT MY GRAND-
MOTHER THAN HER SIL-
VERY HAIR (UNLESS, OF
COURSE, IT WAS HER
FALSE TOOTH!). I LOVED
THE WAY HER VERY FINE
GRAY HAIR WAS GENTLY
PERMED AND LAY TIGHT
UNDER HER HAIRNET IN A
TIDY, FLAT WAVE.
WATCHING HER PUT ON
THE HAIR NET WAS SUCH
AN AMAZING SIGHT FROM
THE HEIGHT OF ONLY
THREE FEET. I DEDICATE
THIS PIECE TO SIMPLE
CHILDHOOD ATTRACTIONS
AND WONDERMENT.

Supplies

80 g* washed, uncarded, lustrous fleece such as English Leicester or Lincoln in natural colors (white, gray, or brown for contrast design)

Washed Wensleydale (for the longer fringe accent)

Pattern (page 116)

Heavy paper

Jorie's Additional Tools (see page 13)

Medium-stiff dish brush

Polyester mesh

Felting kit (page 12)

2-inch (5 cm) diameter plastic pipe

*Purchase a little more wool than necessary so you can select the best staples.

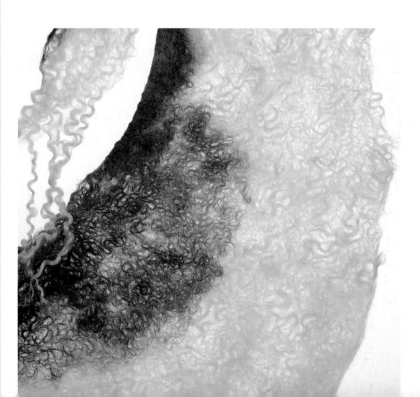

Staples

Wool from sheep with very long, lustrous locks—or staples—is used for this shawl. Make sure that the wool is well washed and free from any foreign matter such as hay or burrs. If the wool feels sticky and has lanolin oil still on its surface, gently wash it before use.

Submerge the fibers in a bath of hot water with a little dishwashing liquid mixed in, and leave them to soak; do not agitate. Check the water and if it is really dirty, repeat the wash bath. Rinse lightly several times in lukewarm water, and roll in a towel to remove excess moisture. Dry thoroughly before starting the project.

In the beginning it may be difficult to tell the tip and root ends of the staples apart. Generally, the tip is a lighter or sun-bleached color and comes to a point, while the base of the staple (the part cut off the sheep) will be denser and have a blunt cut end.

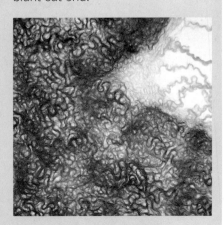

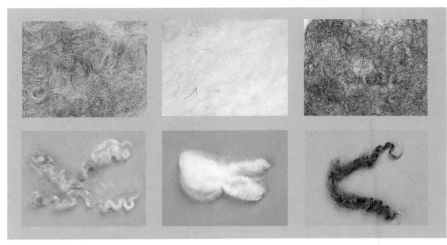

Samples: each sample was made with 5 g of washed wool. The starting size was 8 x 12 inches (20 x 30 cm); the resulting felted size was 5 x 8 inches (12.5 x 20 cm). Left: English Leicester, center: Comeback, and right: Lincoln.

INSTRUCTIONS

1 Enlarge the pattern found on page 116 to 53 x 35 inches (134.6 x 88.9 cm), and trace it onto thick paper. Place the pattern on a table and cover with a larger sheet of bubble wrap or stiff plastic sheeting.

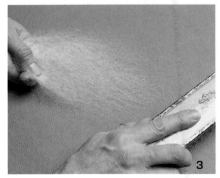

2 Separate the English Leicester staples, dividing by color and length (longer-fiber staples from shorter ones.) If the staples are too thick, subdivide them again by pulling from the tip end only to dislodge a bunch.

3 To realign each staple's fibers, stretch and "snap" the staple several times. Spread the staple open from cut end toward the tip (photo 1). Holding the spread out staple between your two hands, snap it again. Use a medium stiff brush and, while holding the tips, continue to open the staple by brushing the cut ends (photo 2). Turn the staple around and brush open the tips (photo 3).

4 Lay the brushed rectangle of fibers directly down onto the plastic. Brush the next staple and lay it over the first rectangle, slightly overlapping it in an ends-over-tips pattern. You should be able to see the pattern paper clearly through the fibers (photo 4).

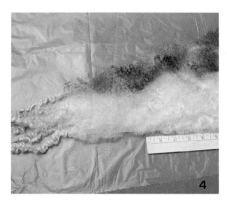

5 After several staples the brush will be filled with the shorter ends. Remove them and save for later. Continue to open, brush, and place the staples, arranging them within the pattern according to your desired color design (photo 5). You will place only one layer of wool to produce this lacy fabric, so consistency is vital. Place four to five narrow staples of Wensleydale at both ends of the shawl to make tassels.

6 Cover the wool with polyester mesh and wet with hot felting solution, as seen in photo 6. Use your hands covered in plastic bags to spread the felting solution until the fabric is well wetted and begins to slip while being massaged. Hand-massage each two-hand-sized area 20 counts. Repeat for the entire surface.

7 Remove the mesh and check the shawl for any sparse areas where it may be necessary to add a bit more fiber (photo 7). If so, use the fibers taken from the brush in step 5, and then apply hot felting solution to the areas with new wool. Cover with painter's plastic, and press out as much air as possible.

8 Flip all of it over and remove the bubble wrap. Do not work the surface with your hands, except to sweep the free-floating fibers back to join with the edges. Lay the painter's

plastic back on top. Wind up the plastic and wool onto the pipe (photo 8). Roll the bundle in a cotton sheet and tie it off. Roll the work 200 counts. Open, rewind, and roll from the opposite end 200 counts. Flip the shawl over and roll again from both ends (for a total of 200 counts from each of two directions). In between rolling, check and repair the sparser areas of wool.

9 Remove the upper plastic sheet and check to see whether the fibers have started to pull together as a fabric. Fill in any large openings among the curls with a sparse cloud of the leftover brushed shorter fibers. Apply hot felting solution and rub gently for 20 counts. Cover with plastic.

10 Fold in thirds and roll the width 200 times. Open and reverse wind from the opposite edge, repositioning the fold lines before rolling another 200 counts. Flip the plastic over and, after repositioning the folds, continue with 200 counts from each edge. Make sure to keep gently stretching out the shawl fabric while it is shrinking so as to maintain its proper shape.

11 Cover the shawl with a plastic sheet, and roll for 200 counts in each of the lengthwise and crosswise directions (rearranging fold lines). Use hot felting solution so you can see slippery white suds within the vacuum of the two sheets of plastic.

12 Open the shawl, ball it up, and throw it onto the tabletop 40 times. Now fold the fabric into roughly a 12 x 18-inch (30.5 x 45.7 cm) rectangle, and roll it up into itself. Close it off in a towel, and roll 40 times. Repeat for the width, then the length. Repeat, totaling 4 x 40 roll counts.

13 Spread open the shawl, apply hot felting solution, and rub the surface with your hands. Continue rolling and hand-working the shawl. If you find a sparse area, stretch neighboring fibers over it or add a few more fibers on top. Don't wait too long to add more short fibers or they may not have sufficient time to entangle well. Work the shawl until the fabric is almost half its original size and the fibers are well connected but still lacy. Occasionally throw the fabric onto the tabletop 20 times, then knead it gently like bread dough.

14 When you have achieved the desired size, wash out the soap. Roll in a towel to remove excess moisture, and leave it to rest 10 minutes in a warm bath with hair conditioner. Lightly rinse and roll the shawl in a towel to remove excess moisture. Steam iron and leave flat to dry.

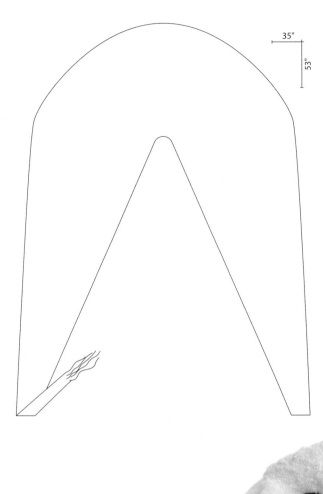

Finishing Options

This shawl can be dip-dyed upon completion, or you may dye the fibers before commencing the project (although undyed fibers felt faster). The basic design can be altered and enlarged for a fuller and more organic shape. Try using the natural colors of the wool to complement your own hair and skin coloring.

WEDDING STOLE

EVERYONE HAS HEARD THE ADAGE: "SOMETHING OLD, SOMETHING NEW, SOMETHING BORROWED, SOMETHING BLUE" THAT ASSURES GOOD LUCK ON A BRIDE'S WEDDING DAY. THIS SHAWL FULFILLS THE SAYING'S CRITERIA IN LOVELY FASHION. BY "BORROWING" THIS DESIGN IDEA, BRAIDING IN A STRAND OF SOFT BLUE MERINO WOOL, AND EMBELLISHING YOUR STOLE WITH BEAUTIFUL "OLD" BEADS FROM YOUR GRANDMOTHER'S WEDDING DRESS, YOU'LL HAVE AN ATTRACTIVE "NEW" STOLE. GOOD LUCK IS SURE TO FOLLOW!

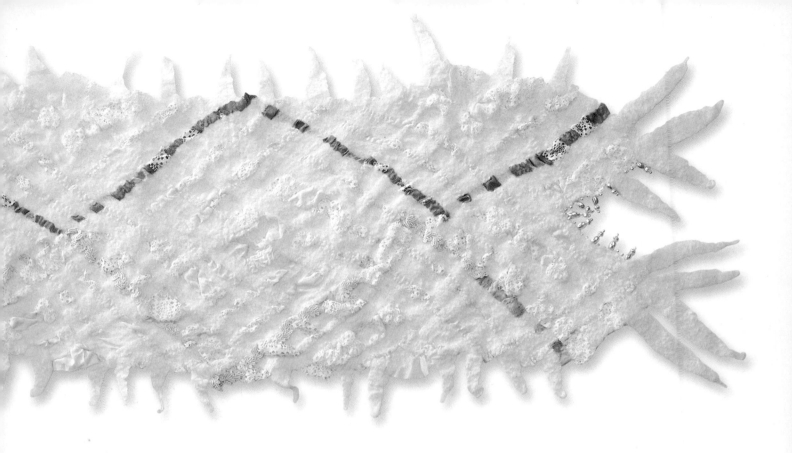

SUPPLIES

Me–80 g white 64 Merino roving

C–Cotton/polyester lace fabric*, cut into eight 1 x 41-inch (2.5 x 104 cm) (or width of fabric) strips (overlap ends and stitch two strips together equaling four strips)

C–Cotton/polyester lace of another variety, 24-inch (61 cm) length

S–Silk, satin, or dense organza cut into strips 1½-inch x 49 inches (3.8 x 124.4 cm) long (equals 98 inches [249 cm] in length when two are stitched together)

Ma–Metallic fabric (or selvedge cut off a fabric or metallic ribbon), ½-inch (1.3 cm) wide; or this may be a "blue" silk ribbon

L–Narrow lace polyester hem edging, ⅜-inch (1 cm) wide x 9 yards (8.1 meters)

Phone book or other wide smooth-covered book (to serve as a weight)

Felting kit (page 12)

Jorie's Additional Tools (see page 13)

Sander and safety equipment (see Selecting a Sander and Sander Safety on page 14)

¾-inch (1.9 cm) diameter plastic pipe

*Lace is expensive, so when possible find a lace fabric that can be cut into strips. This is a chance to use up white remnant laces, ribbons, and fabrics, as well as invest in a few new beauties.

MATERIAL ABBREVIATIONS

Me–64 Merino roving, 60 inches (152.4 cm)

C–Cotton/polyester lace fabric

S–Silk, satin, or dense organza

Ma–½-inch (1.3 cm) metallic fabric or ribbon

L–Lace polyester hem edging

INSTRUCTIONS

1 Separate the Merino roving into twelfths, or as is feasible with your particular roving. Check for consistent thinness in all strands (see Flat Braid Sampling page 38). Carefully pull open each strand until you are able to see the tabletop through it (photo 1). Lay seven strands on a smooth-surfaced table with equal space in between each. Lay the lace and fabric strips in place according to the order. Place a smooth wide weight (such as a phone book) on top to stabilize the strands. Here you are using 15 strands to make each separate fabric length.

Braid Material Order: Me-L-Me-C-Me-L-C-Me-Ma-L-Me-L-Me-Me-S

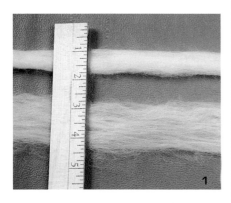

2 Follow the braiding instructions starting on page 38. Try to end the braid so that there are four wool strands in the center, which will become the fringe. Be consistent with your tension, and maintain the width of the braids by marking on the binding of the weight you are using. Make two braids the same length, and try to end each with a wool weft on each outer side and four wool strands in the center.

3 After the initial starting and after you have worked your way out to the edges, remember to *curve* (not twist) the wool strand tightly into place (photo 2). But when working a lace or fabric strand, fold it over itself on an angle (photo 3) and pull it inward and tighter into the edge than the wool, as these materials do not shrink as the wool does. If you need to add on to the lace strands, overlap the ends ¼-inch (6 mm) and stitch them together when necessary. Weave two approximately 8 x 88-inch (20.3 x 223.5 cm) braids (exclusive of fringe).

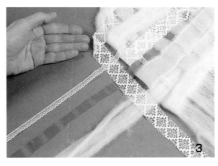

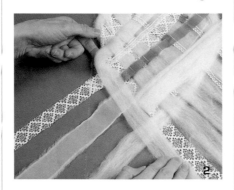

4 Refer to photo 4 to see how to stitch the ends of each of the two braid lengths together so that they will maintain their shape during the felting stage. Cut off the excess length of the ribbons and lace, leaving a small amount to be turned over the outer wool strand and stitched back onto itself.

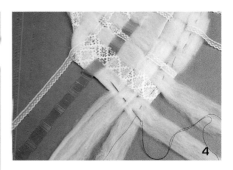

5 Cut the wool strands off at the base of the braid except for the center four (photo 5). If the wool strands are too long, place the weight of your palm on top of one and pull off the excess with your other hand. A single strand layer is often too thin in the final felted fringe, so add an extra strand to each by slipping the ends back up into the braided area.

6 Now you are ready to join the two braids together. To lend extra support to areas where the wool strands of the two braids touch, lay a 4-inch (10.2 cm) tuft of supplemental wool on top and interconnect the two braids on the diagonal in several places (as seen in photo 6 on page 120). Using polyester machine thread, stitch through each edge along the center length of the stole with a blind stitch. Pull tightly, causing the wool to make a dimple (after felting this will disappear, and you will not need to remove the thread if you use the same color as your wool).

7 Check the overall surface of the stole and spread the strands open in areas where there are holes, as shown in photo 7.

8 For more fringe, slip an extra 5-inch (12.7 cm) tuft of wool around the edge of each strand of wool; fold the strand on top of itself (photo 8).

9 Position the stole on bubble wrap and agitate with a sander, following steps 10 through 12 on pages 106 and 107 of the **Father's Day Braided Muffler** project. Be sure to review and follow Sander Safety on page 14.

NOTE: *Although this project is braided in the same fashion as the Flat Braid Sampling on page 38, nearly half the required wool amount will be replaced with lace and strips of airy fabrics. You will be braiding two wide bias bands to be sewn together before the felting process begins. It is difficult to braid very long lengths of strands, so just add on to the strands and work in shorter lengths. I also recommend that you use different laces in the same width so that the repeating pattern will have a fresh look.*

For this project, the length of the roving is more important than the exact weight, so expect to have some wool remaining at the finish.

10 Moisten the stole with hot felting solution, and then roll up the wool lengthwise in bubble wrap and painter's plastic around the plastic pipe. Roll for 200 counts. Open and roll from the opposite end for another 200 counts. Apply more hot felting solution and, with plastic bags covering your hands, rub the surface of a two-hand-sized area diagonally for about 20 counts.

11 Remove the bubble wrap and roll the stole inside the painter's plastic on the same size rod, for two more 200-count sessions, rolling from both ends. Rub the surface diagonally, applying hot felting solution as in the previous step.

12 Roll the stole on itself and then inside a cotton sheet to secure it. Roll about 100 counts; open, and reverse roll another 100 counts. Wring it out and throw onto the tabletop 20 times. Throwing helps pucker the surface and brings out the interesting wool and lace surface effects. Stretch the stole out and, if necessary, throw for another 20 counts. Be careful not to overwork the fabric or you will lose your chance for a soft drape. Check to see if the very center section needs any extra rubbing.

13 Shrink until the inner seam area measures approximately 60 x 10 inches (152.4 x 25 cm) wide. Rinse well in warm water, wring, and soak in a mild acid solution for 10 minutes. Wring out the excess moisture in a clean towel, then steam iron the fringe ONLY. Hang to dry.

14 Further embellish with dear Granny's pearl beads or with felt flowers, if desired.

LEI COLLAR

CREATE A DECORATIVE, LIGHTWEIGHT WOOL FLOWER LEI THAT OFFERS WELCOME WARMTH AND A TOUCH OF SOFT COLOR UNTIL SPRING ROLLS AROUND AGAIN. HERE YOU CAN USE PASTEL COLORS EITHER NATURALLY DYED OR DYED WITH DILUTED ACID DYES. THIS PIECE OFFERS AN ALTERNATIVE APPROACH FOR WORKING IN UNUSUAL SHAPES—A CUTWORK DESIGN IN THE ROUND.

Assorted 64 Merino colors, vegetable-dyed or similar colors with acid dyes in these approximate amounts:

4.5 g color A—chocolate brown (3.5 g for flower, 1 g for three flowers centers)

5.5 g color B—yellow green (3.5 g for flower, 2 g for all stems)

9.5 g color C—beige (5.5 g for larger flower; 3.5 g smaller flower, .5 g for flower center)

4 g color D—pink (3.5 g flower, .5 g flower center)

.5 g color F—total for two mixed greens (for two flower buds)

Assorted novelty yarns (80% to 100% wool/mohair blends only) for flower details

Pattern (page 125)

Heavy paper

Jorie's Additional Tools (see page 13)

Polyester mesh

Felting kit (page 12)

2-inch-diameter (5 cm) plastic pipe

⅝-inch-diameter (1.6 cm) snap

Scrap of fabric to cover snap (dense, yet fine broadcloth in a suitable color to match the collar)

Iron-on interfacing

INSTRUCTIONS

1 Enlarge the pattern found on the facing page to 27½ x 29 inches (70 x 74 cm), and trace it onto thick paper. Place a 42-inch-square (107 cm) sheet of bubble wrap on top of the pattern.

2 Weigh out color A. Thoroughly mix up the direction of the fibers with your fingers. If the fiber length is 3 inches or more, cut it in half or thirds. Lay the wool directly onto the bubble wrap, or work on top of a sketch (photo 1). Press and compact the fibers with dry hands. Once complete, slide the motif off onto the bubble wrap. Repeat for all the flowers, leaving their centers open.

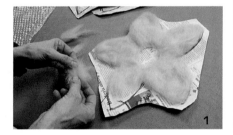

3 Using slightly lesser amounts of wool in the areas where the flower petals join, sandwich the two petals while slightly overlapping the different color layers (photo 2). Since you are only placing one substantial layer of wool into the shape, use the entire amount weighed per flower.

4 Weigh out the center areas of each flower, and work in the same manner as you did for the flower petals. Next, work the areas for the stem (color G, yellow green) that runs around the entire collar. Where it joins to the flower, sandwich it between the flower petal layers, Doing this allows you to have a reversible lei.

5 To make the buds (color F), slightly mix the remaining two greens and then roll them into two small dry balls between the palms of your hands. Separate the wool just below the ends of the stems of both Flower A and E. Push a bud ball into each of the two opened areas so it shows on both sides. The stem color should still wrap around and be connected at the tip (photo 3).

6 Check for even thickness of all the flower petals and centers. Using photo 4 as a guide, cut and lay down various novelty yarns to create details on four of the flowers. Note that the pink flower has five darker pink wool roving flames coming from the edge of the center color.

7 Cover the entire wool area with a net. Sprinkle with warm felting solution, and gently massage the felting solution into the wool, completely wetting all areas. Carefully remove the net. Tidy the edges of all the flowers by sweeping the loose fibers back toward the flower with your fingernails.

8 Place a sheet of painter's plastic on top and push out any air bubbles. Gently flip over the entire package of bubble wrap, wool, and plastic. Remove the top sheet of bubble wrap, and check for consistency of the thickness throughout the flower and stem areas. Apply small amounts of wool to any thin areas.

9 So that either side of your collar can be worn faceup, lay down novelty yarn details on the flowers on the reverse side as you did in step 6. You may choose to repeat the identical details, or lay down completely different ones so that each side shows a unique pattern. Cover with a net and wet the dry areas with warm felting solution. Remove the net.

10 Cover with another sheet of painter's plastic and press out any air pockets. Roll up around a 2-inch-diameter (5 cm) pipe and then inside a cotton sheet; tie off well. Roll 200 counts. Open the bundle, and wind up and roll from the opposite side. Roll for another 200 counts. Open, check the edges of the work, and roll up widthwise this time. Roll 200 counts, and then re-roll from the opposite side for 200 more counts.

11 Apply hot felting solution and massage the surface of the collar. Flip the work over. Using a narrower ⅝-inch (1.6 cm) pipe, roll in all four directions while applying more pressure each time. Cover with a sheet of painter's plastic. Roll 100 counts in all four directions.

12 Repeat wetting and working the surface. Continue to roll the collar inside the plastic sheets until you are satisfied with the size, proportion, and density of the felt. The finished diameter of the lei, depending on the flower shapes, is between 19 and 21 inches (48.3 and 53.3 cm).

Finishing

13 Rinse in hot water several times and leave to soak in a mild vinegar solution for 10 minutes. Roll in a clean towel to remove excess moisture. Steam iron on hot setting and lay flat to dry.

14 Cover the metal snap parts with matching material backed with interfacing, and sew to collar in flower centers in appropriate positions (photo 5).

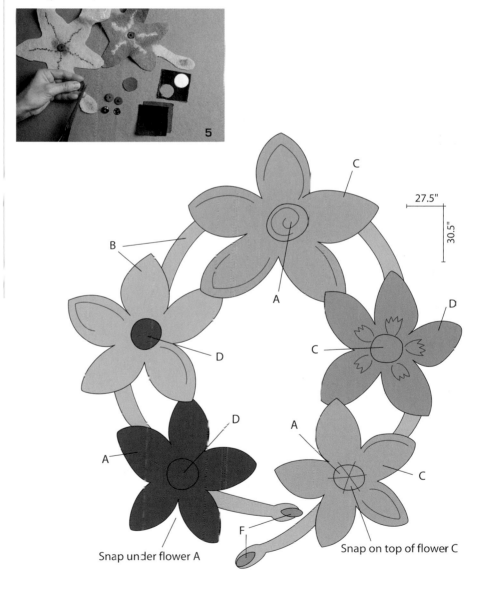

125

THIS LIGHTWEIGHT NECK WRAP HAS EEEN A BIG SIGNATURE SUCCESS STORY FOR JOI RAE TEXTILES OVER RECENT YEARS. HERE THE WOOL IS USED NOT AS A BASE FCR INLAY FABRIC, BUT AS A FORM OF DESIGN EMBELLISHMENT. WEAR ONE NECK WRAP AND CARRY ANOTHER ONE OR TWO IN YOUR PURSE. BY JOINING THEM TOGETHER, YOU CAN QUICKLY MAKE AN ELEGANT EVENING STOLE. AS LIGHT AND DELICATE AS THESE MUFFLERS MAY APPEAR, THEY CAN ALSO BE RELIED ON TO PROVIDE WARMTH WITH FASHIONABLE ELEGANCE WHETHER IN TOKYO, NEW YORK, OR PARIS.

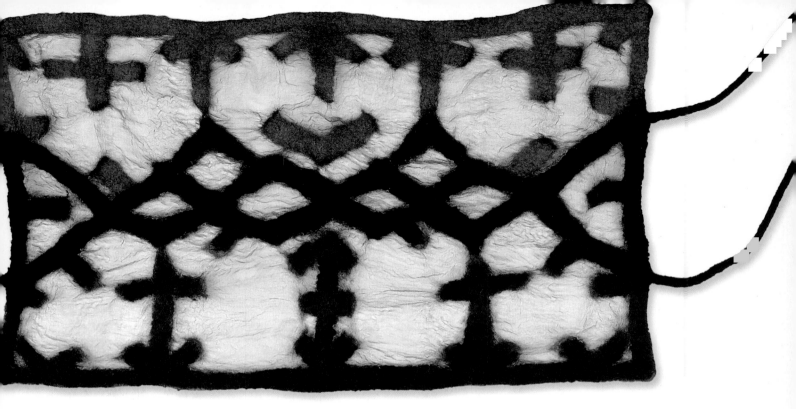

NOTE: *Before choosing a base fabric, inspect your choice for openness of weave, thickness, and also the potential slipperiness of the wetted surface. Most natural fiber-based fabrics, such as silk, cotton, viscose (reconstituted vegetal fiber), and linen once wetted will swell or slightly twist, not allowing the wetted, soapy wool fibers to slide too far before grabbing into the surface. In contrast, polyester or nylon fabrics pose the problem of resisting the wetted wool, which may cause areas of your motif to slide around and felt into an independent fabric before felting to the base.*

With this project, it is recommended to start with cold felting solution so as not to shock the fine fibers into forming a felt fabric before piercing and entangling with the base fabric you have chosen.

SUPPLIES

Silk organza (printed, tie-dyed, or plain), 16 x 26 inches (40.6 x 66 cm)

20 g fine Merino black roving (16 g for design, 4 g for ties)

2 g each of two contrast colors, (such as Yellow Green and Beige)

Cord making supplies (see page 29)

Felting kit (page 12)

Heavy paper

Jorie's Additional Tools (see page 13)

2½-inch-diameter (6.4 cm) polystyrene foam rolling rod

1-inch-diameter (2.5 cm) rolling pipe

INSTRUCTIONS

1 You will need to make two long cords. Subdivide the black Merino roving into eighths of about 24 inches (61 cm) in length, and follow the cord making instructions on page 29, making sure to keep the ends dry throughout the rolling.

2 Enlarge and transfer the diagram on page 130 onto heavy paper. Place the pattern under a larger piece of bubble wrap, with the bubble side down. Center the fabric on the bubble wrap over the pattern, and wet it to keep it from shifting around.

3 Cut the two cords in half to make four, and splay open the dry ends of each. Position them in place on the silk fabric with half of the root on top of the silk, and half underneath, sandwiching and following the pattern (photo 1).

4 Evenly divide the wool top width-wise along the length, into eight or more finer strands. Keep in mind that the narrower you separate the strands from the roving, the easier it is to control finer details.

5 Pull out 10 to 15 small tufts of yellow green wool at a time, and lay them on the tabletop. To create the edges, place each tuft onto the silk fabric, positioning it two-thirds on the fabric, and one-third off the fabric edge so it slightly overlaps the previous tuft. Follow the designated color areas and lay just enough wool so that the fabric is no longer visible (photo 2). Cut the tufts to make square corners, rather than overlapping the ends (photo 3). Add more wool to thin areas, but remember that the goal is to see how little wool is necessary. Lay down the black wool in the remaining two-thirds of the pattern.

6 Cover with the mesh and thoroughly wet with a minimum of warm felting solution. Spread the solution with plastic bag-covered hands. Once evenly wetted, carefully remove the mesh, and use your fingernails to sweep the loose ends of fibers all around the edge back in toward the scarf (photo 2, page 133).

7 Cover with a sheet of bubble wrap, and flip the bundle over . Remove the upper bubble wrap. Repeat step 5 for the reverse side (photo 4). Now use beige on ⅓ of the black area of the reverse side and fill in the remainder of the design with black.

8 Cover with the mesh again, wet well, and then mop up any excess felting solution with a dry towel. Remove the mesh. Lay a sheet of painter's plastic on top, and roll up the muffler lengthwise around a 2½-inch-diameter (6.4 cm) foam rolling rod. Tie off well, and roll for 300 counts. Open, and reverse roll for another 300 counts from the opposite end. Check the edges.

9 Flip the work over and wind it up again along the length. Roll the back side from both ends for a total set of four rolling sessions of 300 counts each. Remove the plastic and lightly soap up the design with baggie-covered hands, massaging in the direction that the wool was laid down. Repeat the rolling set again with a 1-inch-diameter (2.5 cm) rod for 300 counts each, for four sides.

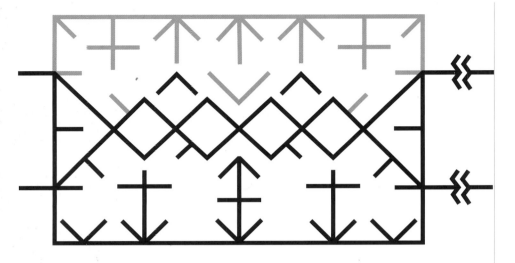

10 Remove the painter's plastic and roll the shorter width for 200 counts, from both sides or top. Flip it over and repeat twice with the other side, with just the one sheet of bubble wrap.

11 If the wool has safely started to enmesh with the fabric, roll into a light ball form and throw 20 times onto the tabletop. Spread out the fabric and, using your palms and lots of warm felting solution, massage the fabric directly on the bubble wrap until it shrinks to the correct size. Occasionally stretch out the felted design areas and the edges. Finished size is about 11 x 19 inches (27.9 x 48.3 cm). Be careful and learn when it is time to stop the process. An overworked fabric will look tired—like a hand-me-down, and you run the risk of distressing away the sheen of a finer silk fabric.

12 Rinse out the felting solution in hot water, then leave to soak in a mild vinegar solution for 10 minutes. Roll in a towel. Stretch out the felt ties. You may starch the fabric and leave it to dry. Steam iron to the proper shape and size, then lay flat to dry.

Here is a chance to use up those mohair yarns you have been keeping. Overlaying mohair odds and ends results in a rich patchwork design. If you choose to use the same yarn brand in several colors, you will get a consistent fabric with fewer surprises. Either way, this scarf will definitely be a one-of-a-kind accessory to complement a favorite outfit or your best winter coat. The look is elegant and, depending on the colors you choose, suitable for either male or female.

CHALK DRAWINGS
MUFFLER

SUPPLIES

Printed or plain viscose, rayon, silk, or any loosely woven or open weave natural fiber fabric*

Assorted Mohair novelty yarns totaling 2 to 3 50 g balls OR 2 to 3 50 g balls of the same quality and brand yarn in several colors (yarn blends must contain at least 90 percent mohair or wool)

Jorie's Additional Tools (see page 13)

Measuring tape and ruler or yardstick

Felting kit (page 12)

1-inch-diameter (2.5 cm) rod

Glass bead (optional)

*Avoid polyester or nylon fabrics, as they tend to become slippery when wetted. Your selected fabric should already have finished edges. I used a natural white, hand-woven Sri Lankan raw silk shawl that I tie-dyed with acid dye.

SCARF MEASUREMENTS

Starting size 19 x 72 inches (48.3 x 183 cm), exclusive of fringe
Finished size 11½ x 57 inches (28 x 145 cm)

NOTE: *Mohair fiber pierces the center base fabric readily when coaxed, and the sheen of the fiber makes a stunning fabric. Check the yarn labels to confirm the mohair content. Many of the new look-alikes actually have no Mohair or wool content in them at all. I myself have been fooled until I read the label! Avoid thin, tightly spun yarns even if they are 100 percent wool.*

Use of the same brand of yarn will result in consistent shrinking throughout the muffler, whereas "patchworking" with assorted yarns may require extra felting in certain areas of the fabric in order for the overall density to be even. Make sure to tie on a change of color or quality yarn when desired.

INSTRUCTIONS

1 Center the fabric on the smooth side of the bubble wrap. Thoroughly wet the fabric with felting solution and stretch it out, forming a rectangle and removing wrinkles.

2 To serve as a guide when applying mohair yarn, lay a measuring tape or ruler along the top length of the fabric and another perpendicular to it (photo 1). Measure the length and width of the fabric, and roughly divide it into finger-span width boxes, each about 4 inches (10.2 cm) square.

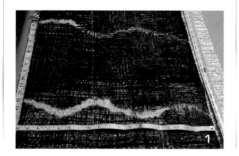

3 Make sure the fabric is very wet. With an ample length of yarn, work in comfortable thumb and forefinger spans to fill each box. Press the yarn into the surface of the wet fabric and, depending on how thick or thin the yarn is, make around nine to 11 zigzags per 4-inch (10.2 cm) box (photo 2). Don't pack the yarn too tightly. Work each box in alternating directions (refer to the diagram on page 135). Keep wetting the surface of the fabric and the area to which you have just applied yarn with warm felting solution to stabilize the yarn.

4 When you have completed the pattern on the top side, cover it with soft polyester mesh netting. Use plastic bag-covered hands to smooth felting solution over the entire surface.

5 Remove the net. Check each box, straightening the yarns with your index fingers, taking the time to position it as evenly as you can within the box (photo 3). Cover the entire fabric with bubble wrap, and carefully flip the muffler over.

6 Remove the upper piece of bubble wrap, and begin placing your pattern on this side. Make sure that if the yarn of the reverse side was laid horizontally, the corresponding section on this side lies vertically (or perpendicularly), so the yarns will be crossing at right angles with the fabric between them. Complete this side as described in steps 2 through 5 (photo 4).

7 With the net still covering the fibers, remove any excess liquid by laying a towel over the surface and patting. This will prevent a wave of felting solution from disturbing the design when you roll it up in bubble wrap. Remove the net, cover with painter's plastic, and press out any air pockets

8 Using a 1-inch-diameter (2.5 cm) rod, roll up the bubble wrap (with the sheet of painter's plastic on top), close it off in a sheet and tie off securely in three areas. Roll lengthwise for 300 counts. Unroll; check the edges for yarns that may have shifted, and rewind from the opposite end. Roll for another 300 counts. Flip the muffler over, remove the bubble wrap, and, while avoiding wrinkling, roll up within two sheets of painter's plastic. Roll for 300 counts in both lengthwise directions.

9 Open and spread out the muffler. Use your hands to rub each square specifically in the direction that the yarns were laid. Use enough hot felting solution so that the fabric slips and slides a little while you are working it, but avoid any wrinkling. Flip the muffler over, and repeat for the reverse side.

10 Continue rolling from each direction and on both sides 300 times. Gently wring out most of the felting solution, check the Mohair fibers are piercing the fabric, and throw the muffler onto the tabletop 40 times.

11 Spread out the muffler again. With well-soaped bare hands, work across the surface of the top half of the fabric in two-hand sections. Rub each section in a back-and-forth motion for 20 counts. You should see some shrinking of the width as you do this. Repeat for the bottom half, then flip the fabric over and work the reverse side in the same manner.

12 Fold the fabric onto itself in thirds. Roll it up over a hard narrow rod, close it off in a sheet, and roll for 30 counts. Open the bundle and refold into fourths. This prevents permanent creases from forming along the previously folded area while shrinking. Wind up the muffler on the rod from the opposite side. Close the bundle off with a sheet, and roll for 30 counts.

13 Squeeze out the extra felting solution, and throw 40 times onto the tabletop. Now use a combination of the various methods described above to shrink the muffler down to size. Continue hand massaging the surface as needed in areas that have a slower felting yarn. Be careful to not overwork the fabric so it will have a nice drape.

14 Once the scarf has reached the desired size, rinse it in warm water several times to remove the soap residue. Squeeze out the extra water. Add a heaping tablespoon (15 mL) of hair conditioner to a half tub of luke-warm water (enough to just cover the muffler), and mix well. Submerge the muffler into the conditioning bath, and press the liquid through the fabric several times for even

application. Let it soak for five minutes, and finish by rinsing it in cold water several times. Spin or wring out the excess moisture, and lay flat to dry.

15 Steam iron the entire piece. While applying steam, use a pair of needle-nose pliers to carefully straighten the edges and perfect the shape of the muffler. Lay flat until completely dry.

If after drying you find areas that have not felted as well as others, simply apply more felting solution and massage with soapy fingers until the square has shrunk in line with the surrounding fabric. Then repeat steps 13 and 14.

16 Embellish the edges of the muffler with glass beads, or tie the fringe in a decorative manner as desired.

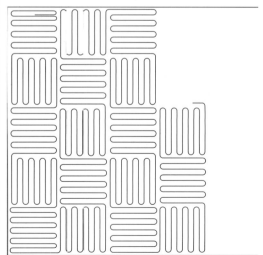

SNOW PEOPLE SCARF

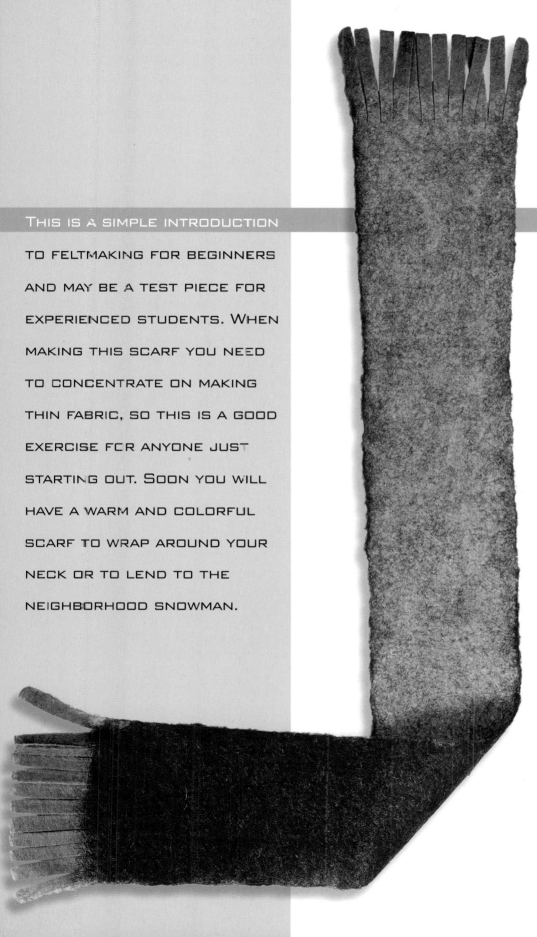

THIS IS A SIMPLE INTRODUCTION
TO FELTMAKING FOR BEGINNERS
AND MAY BE A TEST PIECE FOR
EXPERIENCED STUDENTS. WHEN
MAKING THIS SCARF YOU NEED
TO CONCENTRATE ON MAKING
THIN FABRIC, SO THIS IS A GOOD
EXERCISE FOR ANYONE JUST
STARTING OUT. SOON YOU WILL
HAVE A WARM AND COLORFUL
SCARF TO WRAP AROUND YOUR
NECK OR TO LEND TO THE
NEIGHBORHOOD SNOWMAN.

SUPPLIES

15 g natural light gray 64 Merino

15 g medium brick red 58 crossbred

2 g of green and turquoise blue 64 Merino or 58 crossbred (for the tip details)

Heavy paper

Jorie's Additional Tools (see page 13)

Felting kit (page 12)

1-inch-diameter (2.5 cm) plastic rod

INSTRUCTIONS

1 Draw out a long 7 x 50-inch (17.8 x 127 cm) rectangle on a piece of heavy paper with a thick black marker.

2 Center the paper scarf outline under a piece of bubble wrap (smooth side up). Divide the bright green wool into four sections. Lay them down in the 2 x 7-inch (5 x 17.8 cm) space at one end of the scarf: four fine layers, each perpendicular to the other. Refer to the laying out instructions on page 22 (photo 25). Cut the fibers so they align just up to the edges. Fill in any thin areas.

3 Once the end design has been completed, divide medium red into three sections and lay out in three layers. Place each layer perpendicularly on top of each other and up to the edges of the outline. Keep within the outlines, and use the wool sparingly and efficiently so that each layer is of even fineness.

4 Lay down light gray as explained in step 3, covering the turquoise area but leaving a 2 x 7-inch (5 x 17.8 cm) area of red open at the opposite end. Start in the opposite direction than the last layer of red laid down in step 3 (photo 1). Finish by laying down four fine layers of turquoise in the remaining 2 x 7-inch (5 cm x 17.8 cm) tip area, to complete the design.

5 Cover with a net and sparingly apply hot felting solution, spreading it around with your hand covered in a plastic bag (page 23, photo 26). Remove the net carefully and using your fingernails, sweep the loose fibers back toward the scarf (photo 2). Lay down a thin sheet of painter's plastic. Roll up the bubble wrap and wool onto a 1-inch-diameter (2.5 cm) plastic rolling pipe; then roll that bundle inside a cotton sheet, and secure each end.

6 Begin the rolling session with 100 counts. Apply minimal pressure at the start. Open up the bundle and roll it from the opposite direction, tying off each end. Start the next rolling session of 100 counts. Open the bundle again and flip the "package" over. Repeat rolling from each end but for 200 counts each, gradually applying more pressure with the forearms for each consecutive rolling session. In between sessions, use your fingers or a pair of needle-nose pliers to pull out the dimples in the edges of the scarf, maintaining a nice straight edge.

7 Apply hot felting solution and massage the surface a bit with your soapy hands. Continue rolling in 200-count sessions until the length of the work reaches 5½ x 40 inches (14 x 101.6 cm). Check that the fibers have entangled so well that you cannot see in which direction they were originally laid down. Apply more hot felting solution, and rub the surface with your palms, working the width in narrow sections for 40 rubs back and forth. Do this for the entire length of both sides. Lightly pinch and rub the edges of the scarf to make them firmer.

Finishing

8 Wash the scarf well and leave to soak in hair conditioner bath for five minutes. Rinse in cold water, and roll in a clean towel. Steam iron and hang to dry.

9 After the fabric is completely dry, make the fringe by dividing the width into ⅜-inch x 2½-inch (10 mm x 6.4 cm) long sections. Using a ruler to measure the increments and then drawing the lines with tailor's chalk is helpful. You should have approximately 12–14 fringes. Cut straight lines with long, sharply pointed scissors.

RAINBOW RIBBONS

AFTER COMPLETING THE
INTRODUCTORY SNOW
PEOPLE SCARF, HONE
YOUR NEW COLOR BLEND-
ING SKILLS BY EXPANDING
YOUR SCARF INTO A
LONGER NECK WRAP. THE
COLORS IN RAINBOW
RIBBONS ARE CREATED BY
THE WOOL COLORS SELF-
BLENDING DURING THE
SHRINKING PROCESS. YOU
CAN START WITH BLENDED
COLORS, BUT AS THE
WOOL FIBERS ENTANGLE
AND CONDENSE DURING
FELTING, COLOR MIXING
WILL OCCUR NATURALLY
ANYWAY.

SUPPLIES

3 g each of 58 crossbred in seven colors

15 g bright yellow 58 crossbred (or you may substitute Merino)

Other supplies as outlined for **Snow People Scarf**

INSTRUCTIONS

1 Draw a 7 x 55-inch (17.5 x 139.7 cm) rectangular outline. Divide the width into seven 1-inch (2.5 cm) stripes. Draw dividing lines down the entire length of the pattern.

2 Lay down each of the seven color stripes (using 3 g each). Wet with felting solution and straighten the design areas using a fork (photo 1).

3 Place three layers of yellow wool on top of the stripes. Follow steps 5 through 8 of the Snow People Scarf. For step 9, measure 13½ inches (34.3 cm) from both ends and mark with a pin. Cut the lines of the fabric separating each color into even strips.

ABOUT THE AUTHORS

After studying textile design in the United States and Finland, **Jorie Johnson** was initiated into feltmaking when plunged into a 1977 Scandinavian felt boot-making class. Struck by the immediacy of wool's amazing properties, she hasn't slowed down since. Jorie is the proprietor of the Joi Rae Textiles Studio in Kyoto, where she realizes her attraction to unique textiles by producing felt clothing, accessories, and art works for the interior environment. An invited tutor for international symposiums, she also researches by expedition to Central Asia. Her work is in The Victoria and Albert Museum (London), and she is the author of *Feltmaking and Wool Magic* (Quarry Books, 2006).

Chad Alice Hagen has been exploring hand felted wool and resist dyeing since 1979. Besides this book, she is the author of two other books on feltmaking: *Fabulous Felt Hats* (2005), and *The Weekend Crafter: Feltmaking* (2002), all published by Lark Books. She writes extensively on art and feltmaking and her felt artwork has appeared on the covers of *Surface Design Journal, Fiberarts,* and *Shuttle, Spindle & Dyepot* magazine. She earned her BA and MS at the University of Wisconsin and her MFA at Cranbrook. Her large felt work is in several major collections and she continues to exhibit in galleries. Chad teaches workshops in the U.S. and Europe and maintains a full-time felt studio in Asheville, North Carolina. She also is an avid book collector.

ACKNOWLEDGMENTS

Chad Alice Hagen

Thank you. Thank you very much. This scarf book is a fabulous co-mingling of creative minds. I would like to sincerely thank my co-author, Jorie, for her energy and thoughtful instructions and commentary. Her felt scarves are some of the most professional I have ever seen. I would also thank our stalwart editor, Linda Kopp, for her steadfast hand through the months of writing and rewriting and oops, more rewriting. Art editor Dana Irwin is responsible for bringing all our collected thoughts into concrete book form, and her inspired design makes each page sing. I would also like to thank my cats, Leon and Sweet Pea, for their patience during this writing time and for not throwing up on the manuscript or the computer

Most of all I would like to dedicate my part of this book to my wonderful friend, mentor, and adopted mother, Mildred Voorhees—whose lifelong love of food, reading, and art while raising six fabulous, creative children with her husband Edwin—has inspired me more than I probably even realize. Millie, now in her mid-80s, continues to paint and exhibit her artwork. She is the kind of role model we need more of in this world. Thank you, Millie, for all you have taught me.

Jorie Johnson

Sincere thanks and applause goes to:

Our editor, Linda Kopp, for encouragingly and unflinchingly guiding us to the final print and doing such a great balancing act between two intense artists. I knew Dana Irwin was the right choice for the art direction of this book because I watched her caress our samples and saw her eyes light up. Through her direction, the character of each work is truly revealed to the audience.

Also my appreciation goes to the loyal Joi Rae Textile studio assistants Yoko Sugiura and Atsuko Ikuno.

And lastly, but number one on my felt power list, I'd like to stand up and while clapping, say "Bravo" to Chad Alice for her work ethic, design fun, clarity in teaching, as well as, her creative contributions to advancing the interest of the medium.

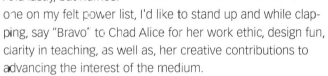

INDEX

3-D forms,
    Ball buttons, 25
    Ball tubes, 26
    Cords, 29
    Ropes, 27
    Tails, 28
Acknowledgments, 141
Art of Feltmaking, The, 8
Ball buttons, 25
Ball tubes, 26
Basics, 10–24
Biographies,
    Chad's, 42–43
    Jorie's, 92–93
Color sampling, 36–37, 100
Cords, 29
Counting stones, 13
Cutting tips, 64
Dyeing,
    Chad's basics, 30–34
    Checking the pH, 30–31
    Chemicals, 30
    Dry dye powder, 34
    Dye baths for resist projects, 33–34
    Hot water bath for thermal shaping, 34
    Jorie's instructions for silk, 35
    Kitchen, 31
    Rules, 33
    Silk fabric, 35
    Soft drink mixes, 74
    Tools, 32
Felting Kits,
    Basic, 12
    Chad's, 13
    Jorie's, 13
    Miscellaneous Tools, 13

Felting Solution, 22
Flat Braid Sampling, 38–41
Gallery, 80–91
Hand carding, 36–37, 100
Hand massaging, 24
Hot plates, 31
Lace, 118
Layout and Felting Basics,
    Chad's technique, 16–20
    Jorie's technique, 22–24
Llamas, 49
Needle felts, 60
Nets, 23
pH, 30
Production line, 28
Projects,
    By Chad, 44–77
    By Jorie, 94–139
Rolling, 23–24
Ropes, 27
Safety, clothing and, 32
Sander, 14
Silk, 35, 95
Soap, 11
Soft drink mixes as dyes, 74
Staples, 114
Stitching, 56
Tails, 28
Technique,
    Chad's, 18
    Jorie's, 22
Tools and Supplies, 10–14
Water, 10
Wetting Procedure, 22
Wool, 10
Worktable and Covers, 11